W9-COH-704

The U.S.
Coast Guard
and Military Careers

Titles in **The U.S. Armed Forces and Military Careers** Series

The U.S. Armed Forces
and Military Careers

The U.S.
Coast Guard
and Military Careers

Judy Silverstein Gray

Enslow Publishers, Inc.
40 Industrial Road
Box 398
Berkeley Heights, NJ 07922
USA

http://www.enslow.com

Library of Congress Cataloging-in-Publication Data

Gray, Judy Silverstein.
    The U.S. Coast Guard and military careers / Judy Silverstein Gray.
       p. cm. — (The U.S. Armed Forces and military careers)
    Includes bibliographical references and index.
    ISBN-13: 978-0-7660-2493-9
    ISBN-10: 0-7660-2493-8
    1. United States. Coast Guard—Juvenile literature. 2. United States. Coast Guard—Vocational guidance—Juvenile literature. I. Title. II. Series.
VG53.G73 2008
363.28'602373—dc22   2006001744

Printed in the United States of America

10 9 8 7 6 5 4 3 2 1

To Our Readers: We have done our best to make sure all Internet Addresses in this book were active and appropriate when we went to press. However, the author and the publisher have no control over and assume no liability for the material available on those Internet sites or on other Web sites they may link to. Any comments or suggestions can be sent by e-mail to comments@enslow.com or to the address on the back cover.

Illustration Credits: Associated Press, pp. 46, 52, 115; Enslow Publishers, Inc., p. 86; Courtesy of Fred Siegel, founder of www.fredsplace.org, p. 108; Illustration courtesy of Northrop Grumman, p. 107; © 2006 Jupiterimages Corporation, p. 19; Library of Congress, pp. 16, 23, 26, 112 (top), 113 (middle), 114 (bottom); Official Coast Guard Photo, p. 12; U.S. Coast Guard Graphic, pp. 72, 73, 112 (bottom); U.S. Coast Guard Photo, pp. 24, 25, 32, 33, 38, 41, 62, 67, 75, 78, 79, 80, 112 (middle), 113 (top and bottom), 114 (top and middle), 115 (top and middle), 116 (top); U.S. Coast Guard Photograph by Petty Officer Second Class Kyle Niemi, p. 10; U.S. Coast Guard Photograph by Petty Officer Second Class NyxoLyno Cangemi, p. 14; USCG photo by PA3 Bridget Hieronymus, pp. 74, 121 (bottom); USCG photo by PA1 Matthew Belson, pp. 3, 55, 100; USCG photo by PA2 Bill Barry, pp. 102; USCG photo by PA2 Chad Saylor, pp. 90, 121 (middle); USCG photo by PA2 James Dillard, p. 42; USCG photo by PA2 Jennifer Johnson, p. 98; USCG photo by PA2 Mariana O'Leary, p. 89; USCG photo by PA2 Tom Sperduto, p. 50; USCG Photo by PA3 Bobby Nash, p. 93; USCG photo by PA3 Dionne Short, pp. 4 (right), 95, 121 (top); USCG photo by PA3 Luke Pinneo, p. 8; USCG photo by PA3 Mike Lutz, p. 105; USCG photo by PA3 Paul Roszkowski, p. 84; USCG photo by PA3 Robert Nash, pp. 60, 116 (bottom); USCG Photo by PA3 Ron Spellman, p. 65; USCG Photo by PA3 Zachary A. Crawford, p. 96; USCG photo by PAC Jeff Hall, pp. 4 (left), 29, 101; USCG photo by PAC Tom Gillespie, pp. 4 (center), 64, 97; USCG photo by PAC Tom Sperduto, p. 68.

Cover Illustration: Associated Press.

Dedication

This book is dedicated to schoolchildren throughout the world so they may know the history of the brave Coast Guard crews serving their country at home and overseas to help protect and defend our nation. It is also dedicated to the memory of Nathan Bruckenthal, whose death on April 24, 2004, while on overseas duty with the Coast Guard, is a reminder of the bravery and importance of human life. Petty Officer Third Class Bruckenthal was assigned to Coast Guard Tactical Law Enforcement Team South, but deployed to the Persian Gulf in support of Operation Iraqi Freedom. He was also assigned to the U.S.S. *Firebolt* as part of Coast Guard Patrol Forces in Southwest Asia. A Damage Controlman for the Coast Guard, he was trained in maintenance, repairs, and fire fighting aboard ship. Bruckenthal was also part of a law enforcement team whose job it was to intercept an Iraqi fishing vessel near the Khawr Al Amay Oil Terminal in the North Arabian Gulf. Though bravely serving their country, Bruckenthal and two petty officers from the United States Navy were killed in action.

Acknowledgments

A special thank you to my father, Harold Silverstein, who has a passion for lifelong learning and teaching. His colorful stories of time spent as a Navy corpsman and his more than fifty-five years of teaching marine biology have inspired my interest in coastal protection. It is from my father I have derived a special joy in participating in something larger than myself. Being part of the Coast Guard allows me to have a front-row seat to history while also allowing me to serve my country.

A special acknowledgment also goes to Fred Siegel, who enjoys sharing his Coast Guard tales and devotion to the service, despite retiring years ago. Both these men understand the importance of serving their country and of passing along important traditions.

Contents

Captain Frank Paskewich, commander of Coast Guard Sector New Orleans, looks out over the ravaged Superdome after Hurricane Katrina. The Coast Guard made many flights along the Gulf Coast in the days following Katrina's aftermath in order to assess the damage.

Hurricane Heroics

United States Coast Guard petty officer Josh Mitcheltree had worked as a rescue swimmer in Alaska and dangled from a hovering helicopter above the sea countless times.[1] But the twenty-three-year-old North Carolina native tackled his toughest mission on August 30, 2005, after Hurricane Katrina ravaged the Gulf Coast submerging entire neighborhoods, killing hundreds of people, and stranding thousands more. No strangers to treacherous weather and unpredictable storms, Coast Guard crews faced new challenges with this dangerous hurricane.

As Petty Officer Mitcheltree looked out the window of his HH-60 Jayhawk helicopter, the earth below him looked nearly flattened. The crew grew silent as they flew along the coast from Mobile, Alabama, to New Orleans, Louisiana. They saw leveled buildings and uprooted ancient oak trees. They heard the radio crackle with descriptions of

▲ Petty Officer First Class Steven Huerta prepares to lift two children in New Orleans into a rescue helicopter after Hurricane Katrina.

the storm's historic and shocking path of destruction. Mitcheltree saw water where city buildings once stood.[2]

The rescue swimmer had heard about the groups of desperate people anxiously awaiting rescue. Facing 100-degree summer heat, difficult rescues from slippery rooftops, and the dangers of tangled power lines, Mitcheltree started planning. "I joined the Coast Guard to help people, and being a rescue swimmer seemed like the most hands-on people kind of job," he said. "In New Orleans, it was no different but it was the hugs afterwards that made it all worthwhile. I was doing something that seemed to make a difference."[3] Many Coast Guard crews who worked in the Gulf Coast region after Hurricane Katrina felt the same.

In a typical year, the Coast Guard rescues about sixty-five hundred people. Yet in the ten days that followed the hurricane, they rescued more than thirty-three thousand people. Mitcheltree said he and his colleagues trained hard to safely rescue people at sea under all kinds of conditions, staying fit by running and working out. He routinely drilled with a crew in the open sea, where wind patterns are fairly predictable.[4] This time, working with other Coasties he had never met before, he watched the wind whip from all directions at the helicopter, which tried to snake its way between buildings. "Everything I was used to doing was a little bit different in New Orleans," he said.[5]

Coast Guard helicopter crews creatively met unusual challenges for hurricane-related rescues. For example, rescuers usually hoist people forty-five to fifty feet into the air from the water. In New Orleans, helicopters had to hover high above rooftops and dangerous power lines so hoists could be as long as 150 feet. In spite of that scary distance, the helicopter was a welcome sight for those whose homes were surrounded by water because it provided a safe return to dry ground. Mitcheltree carefully avoided power lines, trees, and rooftops. Surrounded by nervous but grateful people who had been through a dangerous storm, Mitcheltree realized many needed comforting words up on the rooftops. The noise of the choppers made speaking

▲ A Coast Guard rescue swimmer prepares an elderly man and woman to be transported to safety after Hurricane Katrina.

difficult, so Coasties used hand signals to stay in touch with one another. "When we're in the helicopter, we work as a team," said Mitcheltree. "We're all one unit striving for the same thing . . . safe rescues. It was no different in New Orleans."[6]

Early that first morning, he had prepared for a long day and a slightly overwhelming crowd of people frantically waving from steep rooftops. Arriving on scene, things seemed chaotic as uprooted trees and severed branches covered virtually every surface. Shopping carts and vehicles had landed in treetops at odd angles. Mitcheltree recalled a two-year-old girl who cried as he placed her carefully in the basket that would lift her to safety. As he reassured the frightened child who was separated from her mother, she pulled herself close into his body and closed her eyes, clutching him tightly. Helicopters from different agencies circled the skies everywhere with a deafening noise, as the winds shook the basket the child was in. Once the child was reunited with her mother inside the helicopter, Mitcheltree felt a surge of emotions: "I just kept thinking of how someone I rescued reminded me of someone in my own family," he said.[7] In just one week, Mitcheltree rescued 138 people.[8] His efforts earned him a Presidential Citation and a call from President George Bush. "That was pretty fun," he said. "I felt like the winner of the Super Bowl. The President thanked me and told me he appreciated the work I was doing."[9] Mitcheltree was also awarded the Air Medal for his heroics.

Like many rescue swimmers, Mitcheltree is humble. He said the Coast Guard is full of many heroes and heroines. "The best thing about the Coast Guard is there are so many people doing a lot of good things."[10] On the scene in New Orleans, he recalled advice from a former supervisor who said a rescue swimmer must be the calming factor in the middle of chaos. That advice came in handy as Mitcheltree and other crew members demonstrated their confidence and training. Though the circumstances were unusual, Mitcheltree said the hurricane operations worked well because skilled people worked as a team, despite the wind, high temperatures, and tough challenges of long hoists.

▲ Petty Officer Second Class Scott D. Rady helps a pregnant woman get hoisted into a helicopter from her flooded New Orleans home.

Their work in New Orleans showed the world that the Coast Guard crews are truly the guardians of the sea.

Specialized training is stressed so that Coast Guard crews remain ready to rescue people whose lives are in danger. However, they also perform homeland-security patrols and keep an eye out for polluters. And although the Coast Guard is the smallest of the five armed forces, it has exclusive authority to patrol the waters of the United States. With a diverse and varied history spanning 217 years, today's Coast Guard is a blend of other agencies no longer in existence. Yet, its traditions of lifesaving and maintaining safety in ports remain as important as the Coast Guard's heroics during hurricane season.

Two

Guardians of the Sea

Flexibility has been a hallmark of the Coast Guard since its earliest days. From securing American ports to safeguarding life and property at sea, the Coast Guard has been helping mariners for more than two hundred years.

The Revenue Cutter Service

Following the Revolutionary War, the United States struggled to find ways to generate money to pay off a growing national debt. The first secretary of the treasury, Alexander Hamilton, created a plan to generate money by taxing goods brought into American ports by foreign ships. However, piracy on the high seas and dangerous weather posed a simultaneous threat to commerce and the safety of American ports. Life at sea could be hazardous.

Raised on the island of Nevis in the Caribbean, Hamilton was familiar with smuggling ships that avoided paying taxes. He knew that piracy

▲ Secretary of the Treasury Alexander Hamilton made way for the creation of the Revenue Cutter Service, which was one of the services that combined to become the U.S. Coast Guard.

interfered with trade, financial health, and border security of the new nation.

As early as 1787, Hamilton wrote in *The Federalist No. 12*, "A few armed vessels, judiciously stationed at the entrances of our ports, might at a small expense be made useful sentinels of our laws." Recognizing the need for courageous patrols, Hamilton created America's first maritime police force, called the Revenue Cutter Service. The Tariff Act of August 4, 1790, called for a fleet of ten cutters.[1] By establishing the Revenue Cutter Service, Hamilton ensured the collection of taxes so important to funding the future of America. Often considered the father of the Coast Guard, he also provided one hundred people to assist in collecting taxes on goods entering American ports.

Sometimes called the Revenue Marine, the seagoing police force protected America's coasts. Each ship had a crew of ten, earning about twelve dollars each per month. Hamilton also lobbied to give each man a military rank just as was done in the United States Navy.

Crews conducted inspections of documents such as cargo lists, called manifests, often seizing vessels found in violation of the law. The vital missions given to those first Revenue Cutter sailors meant ships had to be both quick enough to chase larger vessels at sea and yet able to maneuver easily through shallow but busy ports and harbors. Some ships were appropriately named *Diligence* and *Vigilant* for their efforts standing watch, while others were named for Revolutionary War heroes such Adjutant General Alexander Scammell. (The secretary of the treasury at the time, Alexander Hamilton spelled the ship's name *Scammel*, leaving out the second "l.") Still others were named after the original thirteen states, such as the *Massachusetts*. Some of these original vessel names chosen in the early days of the Revenue Cutter Service are still used by the Coast Guard on newer versions of the vessels.

The first commissioned officer of the Revenue Cutter Service was Hopley Yeaton of New Hampshire, who had served in the Continental Navy during the Revolutionary War. (A commissioned officer in the Coast Guard has the rank of ensign or higher.) Appointed on March 21, 1791, by President George Washington, Yeaton was named "Master of a Cutter in the Service of the United States for the Protection of Revenue" and was assigned to the 57-foot schooner *Scammel*.[2]

The history of the Coast Guard has often reflected the growth of maritime interests at home and overseas. Many of the original duties of Revenue cuttermen are an essential piece of homeland and port-security duties today. As the oldest continuous maritime service, the Coast Guard once served as our country's navy. As early as the 1790s, it quarantined ports during outbreaks of diseases, such as yellow fever. The Coast Guard has also provided crews and ships in support of the U.S. Navy during times of war.

Lighthouse Keepers

To make harbors safe for passage at night and in blustery weather, lighthouses were established in 1716 in the British colonies in America. Some had primitive lanterns lit by candles or whale oil, and all were manned by brave volunteers. By 1812, lighthouse keepers operated those lights often using lenses that bent the light to provide better illumination.

After 1822, they began using better magnifiers called Fresnel lenses. The lighthouse keepers often had to summon volunteers to help rescue mariners caught at sea. Tales of brave lighthouse keepers are a rich part of the Coast Guard's courageous and exciting search-and-rescue legacy. Many women often served dutifully, as did war veterans. In 1910, the U.S. Lighthouse Service was created. However, the Lighthouse Service did not officially become part of the Coast Guard until 1939.

The Cape Hatteras Lighthouse in Buxton, North Carolina, was rebuilt in 1870. The Lighthouse Service painted the new structure with black and white stripes so that it would be more easily recognized in the daytime.

The Quasi War

The first chance for the Coast Guard to prove itself in battle came in 1798, during the Quasi War with France. This conflict began after the French seized American ships in protest of the United States' trade with Great Britain. Fought between 1798 and 1800, this was an undeclared sea war. Although France had been considered an ally during the Revolutionary War, they opposed a 1794 trade treaty between Great Britain and the United States. The French began seizing American ships that were trading with the British. In response, the United States Congress authorized the president to arm and acquire up to twelve vessels, and canceled all treaties with France. The Coast Guard cutter *Pickering* captured ten ships, but the war concluded in 1800 when a treaty was signed and French piracy decreased. (A cutter is a Coast Guard ship that is sixty-five feet or longer.)

War of 1812

In the early 1800s, the Coast Guard was tested again when the United States went to war with Great Britain. Americans were upset because British vessels were disrupting American shipping. In what became known as the War of 1812, the Navy prized the fast and shallow-draft Coast Guard ships because they could easily navigate through ports. This war began the Coast Guard's long history of fighting "brown water" wars—naval fights close to shore.

During the war—on the night of June 12, 1813—the Revenue cutter *Surveyor*, with a small crew of sixteen, was captured by the British frigate H.M.S. *Narcissus* after a fierce hand-to-hand combat in the Chesapeake Bay. By then, the courage and expertise of men of the Revenue Cutter Service had become legendary. The official history of the Revenue Cutter Service gave the following account: "Although outnumbered and surrounded by the enemy, the crew did not flinch, contesting the deck with stubborn courage in response to ringing appeals from Captain Travis, who did not surrender his vessel until further resistance would have resulted in useless and wanton shedding of blood."[3]

Also during the war, the Revenue Cutter Service became the first to capture a British ship when the *Vigilant* captured the British ship *Dart* on October 4, 1813.

The Seminole and the Mexican War

In 1832, the secretary of the treasury ordered the Revenue Service to assist mariners in the winter months. The outcome was so successful, that in 1837, lifesaving became a core mission and vital foundation of today's Coast Guard. From 1836 to 1839, the fleet was called on to help fight the Seminole Indian Wars on inland rivers and waterways in Florida. The Seminole were attacking

U.S. Lifesaving Service

Hazardous seas jeopardized the lives of mariners, which gave birth to volunteer lifesaving forces. In Massachusetts, lifesaving stations stocked life jackets, life cars (gear and pulley systems), and occasionally a horse-drawn cart and small lifesaving boats. By 1848, these various stations were located along the Atlantic and Pacific coasts to aid the Gulf of Mexico and the Great Lakes mariners in distress. By 1854, a full-time keeper at each station was paid by the federal government. In 1871, Sumner Kimball became Chief of the Treasury Department's Revenue Marine Division. Kimball convinced Congress to appropriate $200,000 to operate the stations and to allow the Secretary of the Treasury to employ full-time crews for the stations. In 1878, the network of life saving stations were formally organized as a separate agency, called the Life-Saving Service. On January 28, 1915, President Woodrow Wilson signed the "Act to Create the Coast Guard," merging the Life-Saving Service with the Revenue Cutter Service to create the United States Coast Guard. By the time the act was signed, there was a network of more than 270 stations covering the Atlantic Ocean, Pacific Ocean, and Gulf of Mexico coasts, and the Great Lakes.[4]

American settlements that were on their former lands. By 1839, most of the Seminole had been killed, had moved West, or had gone deeper into the Florida swamps.

The Coast Guard's fleet was also an ideal platform for support to the U.S. Marine Corps. These ships contributed to the success of shore battles during the Mexican-American War (1846–1848), which was fought over a land dispute in present-day Texas.

The Civil War

For nearly two decades in the early nineteenth century, the Revenue Cutter Service worked intercepting ships participating in the slave trade. Outlawed in 1808, the slave trade often saw hundreds of African slaves chained in the lower decks of ships. The larger conflict over slavery in the United States soon led to the Civil War between the North and the South.

On April 11, 1861, the cutter *Harriet Lane* fired the shots that signified the beginning of maritime battles during the Civil War. When President Abraham Lincoln was assassinated in 1865, Revenue Cutter personnel were ordered to search ships for the assassins.

As the nineteenth century came to a close, Revenue Service cutters once again expanded

▲ The U.S. cutter *Harriet Lane* operated during the Civil War.

Captain Ellsworth Price Bertholf

Captain Ellsworth Price Bertholf was part of the Overland Expedition of 1897–1898 to successfully rescue a fleet of 273 whalers trapped by ice near Point Barrow, Alaska. Creativity, flexibility, adaptability, and physical stamina—all considered good attributes for people in the Coast Guard even today—led to a team award of the Congressional Gold Medal of Honor. Bertholf led a similar and challenging rescue and relief mission in Russia.

In 1895, he became the first Revenue Cutter officer to attend the Naval War College in Newport, Rhode Island, despite discipline issues while he had been at the U.S. Naval Academy. He had also proudly led the Revenue Cutter Service through establishment of an ice patrol following the sinking of the *Titanic*. Beginning in 1911, Bertholf served as commandant of the Revenue Cutter Service, despite politics that threatened to shut down the small service.

In 1915, when the Coast Guard was formally created, Bertholf was named first commandant of the Coast Guard. His vision of a modern-day maritime military service with many important missions and jobs continues to inspire today's Coast Guard leaders. In fact, the Coast Guard's first National Security Cutter, *Bertholf,* was christened on Nov. 11, 2006, in honor of this courageous and visionary Coast Guard leader.

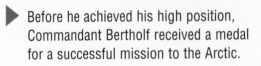

▶ Before he achieved his high position, Commandant Bertholf received a medal for a successful mission to the Arctic.

their protective duties beyond America's coastline, joining their Navy counterparts to successfully blockade Havana Harbor in Cuba during the Spanish-American War in 1898. The United States had gone to war with Spain after a U.S. Navy ship, the U.S.S. *Maine*, exploded in the harbor. During the war, lifesaving stations were also manned as observation posts, providing a critical and useful line of homeland defense.

On January 28, 1915, President Woodrow Wilson signed the "Act to Create the Coast Guard," combining the Life-Saving Service and the Revenue Cutter Service. That historic event marked the beginning of the unique and capable branch of the armed forces known as the Coast Guard.

CAREER PROFILE

Ida Lewis: Lime Rock Keeper, Newport, Rhode Island

Credited with saving at least eighteen lives, Idawalley Zorada Lewis, along with her mother, took over as a lighthouse keeper for her father in 1857. At the time, she was fourteen or fifteen. She served until her death on October 24, 1911.[5] President Ulysses S. Grant visited her after word of her courageous and heroic rescues eventually made it to the White House. In 1879, she became the official keeper of the Lime Rock Lighthouse. In 1924, Lime Rock lighthouse was renamed Ida Lewis Lime Rock Lighthouse, making it the first and only lighthouse named for a keeper. In 1995, the Coast Guard named a buoy tender stationed at Newport, Rhode Island, in her honor.

The Coast Guard issued this poster in 1917 to try to get people to enlist during World War I.

Three

Challenges and Successes

In the twentieth century, the newly formed Coast Guard saw many challenges come its way.

World War I

In April 1917, when five American merchant ships were sunk by German submarines off the American coast, President Woodrow Wilson asked Congress to declare a war because, "The world must be made safe for democracy."[1] As during all previous wars, the Coast Guard's predecessor, the Revenue Cutter Service, was moved under the control of the Navy. In an important move to safeguard the security of ports, the Coast Guard seized enemy merchant ships in U.S. harbors, quickly regaining control of our homeland waterways. Five Coast Guard cutters—*Tampa, Seneca, Yamacraw, Ossipee, Algonquin,* and *Manning*—also sailed to Gibraltar to join the Atlantic fleet. However, after successfully escorting more than 350 vessels, the cutter *Tampa* was struck by a torpedo. It was the largest single seagoing loss of American life during World War I.[2] The *Tampa, Seneca,* and *Ossipee* protected 1,526 merchant ships in 280 convoys, while the *Seneca* rescued 139 survivors from four ships that had been torpedoed.[3]

After the war, with only four thousand members, the Coast Guard patrolled the Alaskan coast and conducted search-and-rescue missions on all coasts of the United States. In 1919, after the Eighteenth Amendment was passed prohibiting the manufacture, sale, or transportation of alcohol, Coast Guard missions were expanded to include enforcement of alcohol-smuggling laws. In 1922, the service rescued three thousand mariners, but rumrunners posed a threat.

Though taxed and undermanned in 1927, the Coast Guard was able to capture the treacherous Horace Alderman, known as the Gulf Stream Pirate, about thirty-five miles off the coast of Florida. While several Coast Guardsmen were transporting a Secret Service agent to Bimini, Alderman attacked, possibly in hopes of keeping federal agents from learning about his stash of Scotch whisky. A gory shoot-out left two Coasties and one FBI agent dead. Alderman was hanged for murder on the high seas on August 17, 1929, at Coast Guard Base #6 near Fort Lauderdale, making him the only person hanged by the Coast Guard.[4]

During the 1920s and 1930s, the Coast Guard rapidly expanded its aviation program.

Ice-Breaking Service

A vital component of the U.S. economy is linked to clear shipping lanes to allow imported and exported goods, such as fuel and oil, safe passage to our ports. Therefore, the Coast Guard's job to keep shipping lanes open stretches today from clearing harbor ice in eastern seaports to icebergs in Alaska. The cutters *Bear*, *Corwin*, and *Thetis* were built to withstand ice and help rescue whalers and fishermen. However, the Coast Guard's first true icebreakers were built in 1926.

Today, the Coast Guard oversees all ice-breaking duties for the military as they steam through hundreds of miles of ice with specially constructed ships.

▲ The icebreaker *Mackinaw* clears a track for commercial ships through the ice of the St. Marys River in Sault Ste. Marie, Michigan, in 2004.

From stopping rumrunners through daily air patrols of Gloucester Harbor to amphibious aircraft landing in open ocean to rescue mariners in distress, the Coast Guard went from a single borrowed seaplane in 1920 to fifty aircraft, seven air stations, and two air detachments in 1938.[5]

In 1935, the United States passed the Neutrality Act. The goal was to provide aid to our allies and prevent arms and ammunition from reaching the hands of what would become the Axis powers—Germany and Japan. While enforcing the Neutrality Act, the Coast Guard seized sixty-four Axis ships in U.S. ports.[6]

World War II

After the United States entered World War II in 1941, the Coast Guard found itself transferred once again to the Department of the Navy. After questioning the crew of a Norwegian fishing vessel, the *Buskoe*, in Greenland, the Coast Guard discovered a large supply of radio equipment that was part of an effort to establish a station for Germany. The *Buskoe* then became one of the two ships taken by Coast Guard icebreakers during the war.

More than eight hundred cutters and one hundred eighty thousand people conducted convoy escorts. Coasties also played a vital role fighting against Germany and Japan. The Coast Guard was instrumental in getting the landing troops ashore at Normandy, France, on D-Day, a pivotal battle that helped the United States and its allies in the fight against Germany. It also helped provide boat-handling expertise for troops in the Pacific. The Coast Guard played a vital role in most major World War II amphibious landings, capitalizing on its boat-handling expertise and bravery in performing search-and-rescue missions.

When the Japanese surprise attacked an American fleet in Pearl Harbor, Hawaii, on December 7, 1941, the Coast Guard ships *Taney*, *Kukui*, *Reliance*, *Walnut*, and *Tiger* actively took part in the battle. As the wave of Japanese fighter jets flew overhead, the American crews fired back. After the Japanese withdrew, the Coast Guard secured the entrance to Honolulu harbor.

After Pearl Harbor, the United States entered the war. In the Pacific in 1942, at Guadalcanal, Douglas Munro, a twenty-two-year-old signalman first class, took charge of a wooden Higgins Boat that was provided to help with an amphibious Marine Corps landing. Maneuvering his boat between enemy fire and withdrawing troops, Munro worked tirelessly to provide enough cover to rescue the Marines. Returning one last time to ensure the safe rescue, Munro took a bullet and died of head wounds. He remains the Coast Guard's only Medal of Honor winner. His medal commends Munro for "extraordinary heroism and conspicuous gallantry in action above and beyond the call of duty."[7] The Coast Guard Cutter *Munro* is named in his honor.

On February 23, 1945 in Iwo Jima, Bob Resnick

▼ Coast Guardsman Douglas Munro fired on Japanese troops to help protect evacuating U.S. Marines at Guadalcanal, an island in the Pacific Ocean.

▲ A Coast Guard-manned ship from the U.S.S. *Samuel Chase* drops off troops of the U.S. Army's 1st Division on the morning of June 6, 1944, at Omaha Beach on the coast of Normandy, France. The invasion was called D-Day and was a turning point of World War II.

of New York not only faithfully stood deck watch, but he also supplied the American flag and a twenty-one-foot steamfitter's pipe for use as a flagpole, to the Marines.[8] As they struggled to hoist it in the infamous volcanic sands atop Mount Suribachi, Associated Press photographer Joe Rosenthal captured the moment, now immortalized at the Marine Corps War Memorial in Washington, D.C.

Across the Atlantic Ocean, the *Bedloe* and *Jackson* patrolled off the coast of North Carolina, searching for German U-boats, or submarines.

SPARs

SPAR stands for "Semper Paratus, Always Ready." The group was created to allow a women's reserve to fill critical shore jobs during the war. Between 1942 and 1946, more than ten thousand women between twenty and thirty-six years of age joined SPAR. From secretaries to mechanics, women filled roles that released men to serve overseas. Lorraine Dieterle was one of many who performed distinguished services. Dieterle took photos of the Coast Guard at work. "My job was to teach the men combat photography, how to stay alive with a camera and a gun on their back, how to block out their cameras, how to mix developer with sea water, how to go through the jungles and how to photograph the landings on D-Day."[10]

While trying to rescue a torpedoed ship, both were sunk in the Great Atlantic Hurricane of 1944, leaving only nineteen survivors, including William Ruhl, who escaped from the engine room of the *Jackson*. "I was proud to serve my country and I learned to love the Coast Guard," said Ruhl, a Pennsylvania native, who scoffs at the notion he is a hero.[9] It is these important sacrifices in a small military service that make the difference in Coast Guard history and might.

During the war, lighthouses and aids to navigation were maintained, key sea channels were cleared of ice, and beach patrols ensured spies did not penetrate our ports. Using dogs and horses, the Beach Patrol kept a lookout on our vulnerable coastline, protecting residents from possible enemies. Coast Guard Captains of the Port ensured cargo was safely transported, laying down the groundwork for port, cargo, container, and marine safety. These expanded duties prompted the Coast Guard to create a women's reserve (SPAR), and beginning in 1943 to rely on a draft to fill shortages in personnel and to integrate African Americans into the service.

The Korean Conflict

The diverse skills of Coast Guard crews offered during peacetime were port security, marine safety, weather-data transmissions, and search-and-rescue skills. Transferring those skills to wartime had become commonplace for the smallest of the armed services. After North Korea attacked South Korea on June 25, 1950, the United States allied itself with the democratic South Korean nation. During the war, twenty-two cutters served at remote weather stations in the Pacific Ocean, gathering important weather data for aircraft. Manning long-range aids to navigation (LORAN) stations located in the Pacific Ocean, Coast Guard crews provided vital information to the other armed services. In January 1953, the Coast Guard played a significant search-and-rescue role when Chinese forces shot down a U.S. Navy reconnaissance plane. The Coast Guard lost five members during this mission.

Back in the United States, the Coast Guard role focused on port protection. President Harry S Truman invoked the Magnuson Act, making the Coast Guard responsible for the national port-security program, a role that endures to this day. Crews checked identification and certification for merchant sailors and supervised the loading of dangerous cargo such as weapons and ammunition.

During the Korean War, from 1950 to 1953, the Coast Guard nearly doubled in size to more than thirty-five thousand members. Broadening peace-time roles to support the other services while America was at war allowed the Coast Guard to become flexible during times of need.

A Sea of Change

In the mid-1960s, the United States aided South Vietnam in its war against North Vietnam. Once again, the Coast Guard was called to wartime duty.

The Brown Water War: Vietnam

Known for expert small-boat handling, the Coast Guard was sought for its skills when a coastal surveillance force was developed for South Vietnam's tangle of rivers in 1965. That year was a turning point for American involvement in Vietnam since military planners had realized rivers were used by the Vietcong to ship large quantities of arms, supplies, and soldiers. Coast Guard boats that could navigate shallow water were needed to detect enemy activity along the South Vietnamese coast. Each day, sixty thousand junks and sampans (boats) crossed the twelve-hundred-mile coast.[1] Intercepting all of the North Vietnamese vessels that were smuggling weapons could easily overwhelm U.S.

Navy forces. Therefore, "Operation Market Time" was expanded to include Coast Guard eighty-two-foot small boats with better maneuverability, inshore capability, and a variety of weaponry. The Department of Defense felt Coast Guard involvement in surveillance and coastal defense would mirror their role in the United States and improve the overall effectiveness of U.S. naval forces.

During the first month of operation, Division 11

Members of a Coast Guard crew inspect a fishing boat during the Vietnam War. Sometimes, North Vietnamese troops disguised their boats as fishing vessels.

boarded eleven hundred sampans, inspected more than four thousand small boats, and established blockades to improve security for South Vietnamese and American forces.[2] These Coast Guard boats also provided vital ongoing medical evacuation, gunfire support, and transport for Special Forces troops during war. They operated more than 70 percent of their time in country, capturing tons of enemy weapons and supplies.[3] Working with the Navy, the Coast Guard provided critical protection for the South Vietnam coastline, harming the enemy's efforts to resupply its forces.

Environmental Missions

During the decades following the Korean War, a series of environmental protection laws were passed. Coast Guard missions were expanded to include environmental protection, commercial fishery protection, and marine environmental response. That created a skilled workforce of environmental protectors capable of ensuring the safety and health of the coastal zone. With duties ranging from patrols that ensure the health of fish species to oil-spill prevention and clean up, Coast Guard marine-science technicians oversee pollution response and preparation. They also inspect cargo and containers to ensure environmental and safety laws are followed. Every day, Coast Guardsmen and women board ships to inspect cargo, check packed containers in port, test water samples, maintain navigational signs, and patrol the coast for boaters who may need help.

As protectors of the coast, Coast Guardsmen still help maintain healthy oceans, rivers, and fishery stocks. Sometimes, the Coast Guard enforces fishing regulations by boarding ships to measure the catches and to educate crew members about any fishing bans.

However, conservation duties are nothing new to the Coast Guard. In 1822, Congress ordered the service to help stop the cutting of live oak trees in Florida. To enforce this law, crews had to maneuver through winding, narrow inland waterways to halt the clear-cutting of the hardwoods.

In 1973, the International Convention for the Prevention of Pollution by Ships set the world's first standard for oceans. Today, the Pew Report discusses what can be done to save the oceans. The Coast Guard is central to ensuring the health of our oceans.

The 1973 legislation was helpful when, in 1989, the *Exxon Valdez* ran aground, spilling more than 10 million gallons of oil into Prince William Sound near Alaska. The Coast Guard helped assist and direct cleanup that took more than 450 boats to cover more than 350 miles of coastline.[4] By inspecting vessels, the Coast Guard tries to prevent oil spills and pollution incidents. When they occur, however, Coast Guard marine-safety teams are there to contain the flow of oil and to clean shorebirds and the coastline.

▲ Coast Guardsmen steam blast rocks soaked in crude oil from the leaking tanker *Exxon Valdez*.

A Coast Guard Tragedy

Sometimes, crews muster courage and bravery to face unknown or unanticipated dangers, even during peacetime. Homeported in Galveston, Texas, the 180-foot buoy tender *Blackthorn* had just completed an extensive shipyard overhaul in the port of Tampa, Florida, when it headed out to return home. At 8:20 P.M. on January 28, 1980, the *Blackthorn* collided with the 605-foot oil tanker S.S. *Capricorn* near the Sunshine Skyway Bridge in St. Petersburg, Florida. As the tanker's seven-ton anchor became embedded in *Blackthorn*, the cutter twisted and sank within ten minutes, taking with it twenty-three of

41

▲ The *Blackthorn* monument at a Coast Guard base in Galveston, Texas, bears the number 23, signifying the number of crew members lost when the vessel sank on January 28, 1980, near St. Petersburg, Florida.

the fifty crew members. The bodies were recovered and buried.

Eventually, the rusting *Blackthorn* was raised and towed out into the Gulf of Mexico where it now lies some twenty miles off Clearwater, Florida, as part of the Pinellas County Artificial Reef Program. *Capricorn*, which suffered only minor damage and no loss of life, was used for scrap in the 1980s.

The principal responsibility of a buoy tender is to service aids to navigation. However, the *Blackthorn* had also been used as an icebreaker on the Great Lakes and in various rescue and salvage operations—including the search for survivors of National Airlines Flight 470 in February 1953.

A stately granite memorial that commemorates the largest peacetime loss of life for the Coast Guard was dedicated January 28, 1981. It is located at the north base of the Sunshine Skyway Bridge where an annual memorial ceremony is held at Blackthorn Memorial Park.

The Mariel Boatlift

Between April 15 and October 31, 1980, a mass exodus of freedom-seeking Cuban refugees were allowed to leave Cuba after President Fidel Castro opened the gates to prisoners, drug addicts, the poor, the mentally ill, and the sick, among others. Leaving from Cuba's Mariel Harbor, the refugees commandeered rickety and sometimes leaking vessels on their way to the Florida Straits. Many struggled to keep their boats afloat. Most of the "Marielitos" landed in Miami, and some were brought to Indiantown Gap, Pennsylvania; Fort McCoy, Wisconsin; and Fort Chaffee, Arkansas, for processing.

Nearly 125,000 Cubans arrived on the shores of the United States in seventeen hundred boats. The rescue operation nearly overwhelmed Coast Guard crews, who worked to ensure the safety of the inexperienced mariners. By May, two Navy amphibious warfare ships arrived to help the Coast Guard patrol the seas, searching for capsized vessels and struggling swimmers. Each day, the Coast Guard conducted four air patrols in the waters closest to Key West, Florida, and Cuba, aided by help from their Navy counterparts. The Seventh Coast Guard district commander maintained tactical control, while Rear Admiral Warren Hamm, U.S. Navy, controlled the middle waters.

Vigilantly monitoring the overloaded boats raised continual safety concerns. On May 7, 1980, Admiral John B. Hayes held a news conference discussing safety concerns raised by the "freedom flotilla." Hayes cited the *Dr. Daniels* incident, a tug that arrived in Key West with approximately six hundred refugees on board with lifesaving equipment for only one third of the people. Concerned about a maritime tragedy, he appealed to the Cuban government in the interest of safety and humanitarianism.

Coast Guard officials met with other agencies on May 10, 1980, to plan a strategy for handling humanitarian and legal issues raised by the influx of boats on American shores. That is when the focus shifted from search-and-rescue operations to law enforcement. Using high-frequency radio broadcasts, the Coast Guard announced it was illegal to transit in an unauthorized vessel and pick up people. Vessels with gross safety violations were escorted into port until violations were corrected. Commercial vessels carrying large numbers of immigrants without visas were detained until collateral for fines was produced.

An overloaded boat capsized on May 17, 1980, and many occupants drowned. Reports from Mariel were dismal. Refugees said the harbor had turned into a police state. At gunpoint, the vessel *Atlantis* was ordered to take 354 refugees with only eighty lifejackets aboard. The Coast Guard cutter *Dallas* responded to a call for help and escorted the fishing vessel to Station Key West in Florida.

"The United States Coast Guard and the Navy have saved thousands of lives during the past seven weeks," said President Jimmy Carter. "I join every American in congratulating both organizations for their good work. We could not continue to permit this unsafe and uncontrollable flotilla to continue."[5]

In early June, the Coast Guard Commandant requested and received presidential permission to call up reservists for up to six weeks. This historic move seamlessly integrated the work of Coast Guard reservists, active duty, and auxiliarists into a lifesaving and port-security operation. By June 30,

▲ A shrimp boat arriving from Mariel, Cuba, is packed with Cuban refugees as it lands at Florida's Key West Naval Base on April 30, 1980.

1980, six hundred Coast Guard reservists had been called-up throughout the nation. The state of Florida was especially taxed as it was a critical arrival point for boats coming from Cuba, straining to stay afloat. Even today, lingering reminders of the boatlift remain. Many Marielitos have become productive U.S. citizens—one even joined the Coast Guard for a stint. But the vast number of people Castro sent to U.S. shores was an unprecedented act by a Third World country. For the men and women of the U.S. Coast Guard, the Mariel Boatlift remains the most dramatic international event involving thousands of hours, one of the largest call-ups of reservists in peacetime, and an extraordinary challenge to Coast Guard resources. And Coast Guard leaders still keep a watchful eye out for an increase in Cuban migrants reaching American shores. Although dealing with migrants is often dangerous, Coasties remain dedicated to rescuing boaters in distress.

Five

Changes in the Air

The Coast Guard of the twenty-first century continues its tradition of protecting the American coast from a variety of dangers.

Still an Environmental Guardian

Coast Guard teams continue to learn about and train to contain oil spills to protect ocean wildlife and coastal wetlands. Through the use of highly technical instruments and staff at their renowned research and design facility in Connecticut, they can detect the origin of a spill just as one is able to link a footprint to a shoe. Careful study and gathering of evidence helps Coast Guard teams pinpoint the ship that spilled the oil, even once it has left the scene.

The Coast Guard also has a National Strike Team that can fly out to manage spills and other environmental disasters. This team was on duty when the shuttle *Columbia* broke up in January

2003 over Texas and other states. A similar team, called the Gulf Strike Team, responded to Boca Raton, Florida, in October 2001, when anthrax was detected in the American Media, Inc. (AMI) Building. Using reservist members with civilian job skills, the team from Mobile, Alabama, displayed world-class knowledge and abilities while collaborating with other environmental agencies.

Search and Rescue

The Coast Guard continues to train for and perform critical lifesaving missions referred to as search and rescue (SAR), steeped in two centuries of training and traditions. In 2003, the lives of more than 5,100 mariners were saved by brave boat and aircraft operators.[1] By law, the Coast Guard is required to respond to boaters in distress out to twenty nautical miles at sea. However, updated technology is improving the Coast Guard's ability to receive important radio transmissions even in poor weather and with aging radios. The goal is a safe, swift, and successful rescue, and a pinpointed location of the vessel in distress helps the Coast Guard accomplish these goals. The Rescue 21 Project includes the use of towers to help identify the position of boaters within one or two degrees. This cutting-edge technology allows the Coast Guard to track its own boats.

As the Coast Guard continues to implement newer radio systems, it also encourages boaters to

▲ Petty Officer Kevin Post holds a scared three-year-old, Johnny Dudek, after rescuing him from a sinking vessel in Horseshoe Cove at Sandy Hook, New Jersey.

use EPIRBs (Emergency Position Indicating Radio Beacons) that can attach to a life vest or a boat in case a vessel capsizes. Boaters can also get free vessel-safety checks from the Coast Guard Auxiliary and can choose from a variety of boating-safety classes to strengthen their knowledge of boat handling. These can now be taken online or in a classroom. Education helps boaters better cope with emergency situations until the Coast Guard arrives on scene.

Because the Coast Guard patrols more than ninety-five thousand miles of coastline, it is more prepared than ever before to juggle many missions simultaneously. While scanning the shoreline and ports for telltale signs of smuggling activity, the crews pay close attention to signs of boaters in distress. From the earliest days of piracy on the high seas, the Coast Guard has developed systems of detection. Today, these include random boat boardings that allow crews to gather information, the instruction and education of boaters about safety equipment such as life vests and flares, and safety inspections of a vessel. Their visibility helps prevent accidents at sea and adds a measure of security to ports. Sometimes, divers and robots are used to inspect the underside of boats, bridges, and ports. Recently, Coast Guard auxiliarists have also begun lending a uniform presence to docks and ports as part of Operation "On-Guard." As they walk the docks, this heightened visibility allows for extended coastal protection and boater safety.

Humanitarian Tradition Continues

While the Coast Guard manages to enforce safe boating environmental regulations and laws, there is a true humanitarian component in all the work it does.

Nowhere is that more evident than in the operations aimed at rescuing migrants lost at sea. Juan Reyes, age forty-nine, recognized that important ingredient as he addressed the crew at Sector Field Office Moriches on eastern Long Island. Relaying details of a rescue at sea in 1965, Reyes gave the perspective of a nine-year-old boy sharing a small boat with thirty-three others. Poised to step aboard

▲ The Coast Guard still rescues refugees trying to come to America. Here, a group of Cuban rafters float next to the *Drummond* about forty miles south of Key West, Florida, on August 23, 1994.

a Coast Guard boat for the first time in forty years, Reyes told the crews their bravery makes a difference in the lives of many. Reyes was the nine-year-old boy he spoke of and now serves as a director within the Department of Homeland Security, where he oversees environmental programs, including those run by the Coast Guard. The speech was an emotional moment for the crew and for Reyes that underscores the importance of protection of life and property at sea.

Movement to a New Agency

During the late 1700s, the Coast Guard was part of the Department of Commerce since its duties focused primarily on trade and economic stability of the young nation. In 1967, President Lyndon B. Johnson moved the Coast Guard into the Department of Transportation, although it remained one of five military branches. Protection of commerce was still a major role played by the seagoing service as it ensured the safety of marine transportation and the free flow of trade.

Although the Coast Guard is only about the size of the New York Police Department, about thirty-eight thousand members, it is notable for its ability to accomplish complicated tasks under extreme pressure. Nowhere was that more evident than in the ports of Boston, New York, and Washington, D.C., when terrorists hijacked four aircraft and struck the World Trade Center and the Pentagon on

September 11, 2001. After this history-changing tragedy, the Coast Guard helped secure the ports while the United States braced for more attacks.

By 2003, expanded missions and changing global situations brought the Coast Guard even more attention in the United States. Homeland-security missions were easily folded into port security, law enforcement, marine environmental protection, and search-and-rescue missions.

It was no surprise then when, on March 1, 2003, the Coast Guard was moved into the newly created Department of Homeland Security. The agency was created to deal with future threats to the United States. Because the Coast Guard is used to having many duties, it emerged as a beacon for the agency because it could respond so well and so rapidly to many new challenges. Reservists who staff the Strike Teams provide chemical and scientific expertise, while public-affairs expertise allows the Coast Guard to teach other agencies how to handle disaster response.

Global War on Terror

In the early hours of April 24, 2004, Petty Officer Third Class Nathan Bruckenthal prepared to board a vessel off the coast of Iraq, with a crew of Navy sailors and one other Coastie. It was a trap—as they approached the vessel, it blew up. The explosion killed Bruckenthal and two Navy sailors. Since port security in the Mideast is a component of an overall

▲ Boatswain Mate Second Class Melissa Steinman maneuvers a transportable security boat during a high-speed patrol while Machinery Technician Second Class Mike Ransdell keeps a lookout for possible threats.

plan for coastal security worldwide, the dangers crews face are part of the equation. Bruckenthal was afforded a stately military funeral at Arlington National Cemetery in Virginia, but his legacy inspires other brave men and women of the Coast Guard.

In the clear waters off Ash Shuaiba, Kuwait, Boatswain Mate Second Class Melissa Steinman expertly maneuvered her boat, her eyes darting quickly around the brightly lit horizon. Boat driving is nothing new for Steinman, from Port Security Unit 307 based in St. Petersburg, Florida. She has manned the helm in waters off Florida and Guantanamo Bay, Cuba. Her assignment in the Mideast differed a bit, but she understands the importance of securing foreign harbors. Steinman is vigilant and knows all too well the dangers of working overseas. The loss of Coast Guardsman Nathan Bruckenthal remains painfully fresh in the minds of Steinman and her shipmates. As the first Coastie killed since the Vietnam conflict, Bruckenthal inspired her unit, and his death placed it on a more heightened alert. Even as the Coast Guard faces shifting missions, it trains continuously to refine centuries worth of skills in law enforcement and coastal protection.

The credible work Coast Guard crews perform has received more focused attention since terrorists struck on American soil on September 11, 2001. The entire Coast Guard has displayed admirable adaptability and flexibility, said its leaders. That is nothing new for a military organization that has changed and remolded several times during its two centuries of history. It is now more capable of responding and is better able to protect the coast both at home and overseas.

For example, port-security units deploy to harbors and ports overseas by request. Staffed primarily by reservists, an efficient twenty-four-hour mobilization allows units to provide waterside security in foreign ports in such areas as the Persian Gulf, Haiti, Cuba, and Bahrain. Each unit is staffed by at least one hundred people with quick boats and an array of specialized law enforcement and weaponry training. Their focus is harbor defense. Marine safety and security teams are staffed primarily by active-duty Coasties, and they respond to coastal security needs at home.

A Team of Many

Workers are needed to deploy teams. From lawyers preparing wills to education officers transferring students to online courses, the Coast Guard ensures its crews are ready to serve. Health Specialist First Class Giovanni Nieves works in the clinic at Air Station Clearwater. A second generation Coast Guardsman with two brothers that also serve, he is responsible for readying crews for critical missions overseas. One of the things he does is help fellow Coasties get regular checkups, including visits to the eye doctor and dentist, before they go on their missions.

Maintaining navigational aids, cleaning oil spills, search and rescue, meal preparation, law enforcement, radio communications, aircraft repair, drug enforcement, and boat driving—whatever the challenge, Coast Guardsmen are dedicated to both looking out for one another while also protecting the coast and the American public. Sometimes, they are called on for more specialized missions.

Coast Guard Creed

The Coast Guard Creed was written by Vice Admiral Harry G. Hamlet, who was commandant of the U.S. Coast Guard from 1932 to 1936. It is known by all Coast Guardsmen.

I am proud to be a United States Coast Guardsman.

I revere that long line of expert seamen who by their devotion to duty and sacrifice of self have made it possible for me to be a member of a service honored and respected, in peace and in war, throughout the world.

I never, by work or deed, will bring reproach upon the fair name of my service, nor permit others to do so unchallenged.

I will cheerfully and willingly obey all lawful orders.

I will always be on time to relieve, and shall endeavor to do more, rather than less, than my share.

I will always be at my station, alert, and attending to my duties.

I shall, so far as I am able, bring to my seniors solutions, not problems.

I shall live joyously, but always with due regard for the rights and privileges of others.

I shall endeavor to be a model citizen in the community in which I live.

I shall sell life dearly to an enemy of my country, but give it freely to rescue those in peril.

With God's help, I shall endeavor to be one of His noblest Works . . .

A UNITED STATES COAST GUARDSMAN.[2]

The G8 Summit and Hurricane Relief

At the G8 Summit on Sea Island, Georgia, in 2004, the Coast Guard presence allowed for heightened security while also maintaining the safe passage of commerce and cargo through northern Florida and southern Georgia. Coast Guard reservists helped plan the massive event, ensuring the safety of bridges and harbors in Jacksonville, Florida; Savannah, Georgia; and Jekyll Island, Georgia, while leaders of the world met to hammer out trade and economic agreements. Establishing an armory and several command centers allowed the Coast Guard to use its best people and training to oversee the massive security operation. Planning teams pored over possible terrorist scenarios for months, working closely with other federal, local, and state agencies. Aids to navigation were inspected, the underbellies of bridges scanned and tested, and patrols stood watch round the clock. Many credit the planning and flexibility of Coast Guard crews with the success of the security operation.

Later that summer, Coast Guard crews fanned out across the southeastern United States to assist in disaster recovery in the aftermath of five turbulent hurricanes. Watch standers were busy putting out notices to mariners to be certain all boaters understood the hazards at sea. Aids to navigation teams checked dayboards and buoys to ensure navigational aids on the water were accurate and pointing in the right direction. Coast Guard crews

▲ Chief Warrant Officer Mike Spute hangs on the side of a boat while on a mission inspecting a bridge for explosive devices during the G8 Summit on Sea Island, Georgia.

helped one another and the American public. From Punta Gorda, Florida, to Alabama, Louisiana, and Texas, stories of individual and team sacrifice once again set the Coast Guard apart as courageous rescuers working hard in spite of storm damage to their own stations and homes. It is this spirit and dedication under the most terrifying circumstances that makes being in the Coast Guard gratifying and rewarding.

That teamwork was evident in January 2005 when the Super Bowl was played in Jacksonville, Florida. Culminating in a successful event, the security plans used at the G8 Summit were tweaked and changed, in another display of Coast Guard innovation.

The Inside Scoop

How is this effective force organized? And what is it like to be in the Coast Guard? Many young men and women have wondered the same things. Today, some of them are part of the many faces of the Coast Guard.

▲ This cadet is ready for a parade at the Coast Guard Academy.

Six

The Faces of the Coast Guard

Coast Guard stations are located from Maine to Guam with some limited overseas assignments. Enlisted men and women work in buildings, on ships and aircraft, and at small boat stations.

Enlisting in the Coast Guard

Military life includes wearing a uniform, adhering to dress codes and traditions, and using respect in addressing officers and superiors.

Requirements for applicants include:

- American citizenship or legal immigrant status with permanent residency
- Being between seventeen and twenty-eight years of age with a high school diploma or GED
- Physical requirements that include height and weight proportions and good vision and hearing
- Minimum scores or higher on the Armed Forces Vocational Aptitude Battery test

Recruits line up on their first full day of boot camp.

Recruits are sent to boot camp for eight weeks at the Coast Guard Training Center in Cape May, New Jersey, once a contract is issued and signed. The contract provides the details of pay, rate and rank, G.I. Bill education benefits, military clothing allowance, and money for housing, food, and board.

In boot camp, recruits undergo classroom instruction and learn first aid, weapons handling, seamanship, shipboard fire fighting, safety, survival in water, and nautical terminology.

Promotions

Enlisted Coast Guardsmen are eligible for promotion after they complete on-the-job training and check off qualifications that include professional military requirements and job specific duties. Biannual evaluations outline career-development paths. Once in the Coast Guard, there are several paths for promotions.

Officer Candidate School

Competition for Officer Candidate School (OCS) is tough and requires that the candidate:

- Have a college degree or be a senior in college ready to graduate
- Have at least a 1,000 score on the SAT or 21 on the ACT
- Be a U.S. citizen between twenty-one and twenty-six years old

Reservists also may attend OCS.

▼ Members of an Officer Candidate School class dress in uniform for a competition.

Coast Guard Academy

Founded in 1876, the Coast Guard Academy was built at its current site in New London, Connecticut, in 1932. Unlike other military branches, the Coast Guard requires a high grade-point average and good SAT scores as opposed to a congressional appointment for admittance into its academy. A challenging four-year curriculum includes marine engineering, naval architecture, marine and environmental science, government, and management. The academy has a higher percentage of pilots than the United States Air Force. Eligibility requirements include:

- A letter of recommendation from a coach and an English and math teacher
- Successful completion of a rigorous physical-fitness test
- Having no debt and being unmarried
- Being seventeen to twenty-two years of age
- Having graduated high school or passed a GED test with good SAT scores (There are six thousand applications annually for three hundred positions.)
- Completion of an interview

Seven weeks before the first academic year starts, cadets transition into the lifestyle of military conditioning, swimming, and skills. They spend one week sailing aboard the cutter *Eagle*. Leadership is also emphasized for academy cadets.

The Barque *Eagle*

Since 1947, Coast Guard Academy cadets have boarded a 295-foot, three-masted barque called the *Eagle*. With its twenty-three snowy white sails, this ship is where cadets begin their training at sea. Voyages aboard this tall ship are a heady introduction to a seagoing tradition.

Cadets practice using a sextant for navigation, rigging the sails, tying knots, and swabbing the decks. During the first summer before the academic year starts, cadets have a one-week taste of naval tradition. Future summers include lengthier cruises for these willing cadets.

The *Eagle* was a war prize from Germany following World War II. Built in 1936 as *Horst Wessel* in Hamburg, Germany, it served as a training vessel for German sailors. For fifty-nine years, it has been a floating classroom providing cadets with problem-solving, leadership, and seamanship opportunities that mirror the most impressive naval traditions.

◄ The Coast Guard cutter *Eagle* sails off the coast of Puerto Rico.

Feeding the Crew

Coasties serve all over the nation and the world, sometimes in remote stations. That often makes it a bit more challenging to accomplish basic tasks, such as grocery shopping for food, or "chow." Many stations have galleys (kitchens) with cooks that prepare meals for an entire crew. The challenge at sea and shoreside is in being creative with what is in the ship's stores (storage).

Morale events such as ice cream or pizza parties help crews maintain a positive attitude. While on long deployments, morale often centers around mealtime or snacks. A food-service specialist learns about food prep while at sea, ordering, cooking, and creating special garnishes to adorn the food for special occasions. Coast Guard events often call for nautical themes, and cooks sometimes whittle carrots and green peppers into palm trees on small islands of lettuce and carved radishes.

Sometimes crews will barbeque fish to encourage more interaction. However, most agree it is challenging to please an entire crew of people while cooking in extremely tight quarters. Even the diners have some challenges of their own, such as keeping a coffee cup steady while on board a ship traveling through rough seas. For many crews, it is just part of the excitement of being in the Coast Guard.

▲ Coast Guard recruits wait for food in the galley at the Coast Guard Training Center in Cape May, New Jersey.

The Coast Guard Reserves

The Reserve Act was passed in 1939, creating a civilian-based force of the Coast Guard. They were charged with extending the active-duty component but also with developing public awareness of boating safety and good seamanship.

In 2003, more than 25 percent of the reservists were on active duty in an effort to help the Coast Guard keep up with expanding missions. For many, the extra work meant also juggling civilian jobs; but with the accessibility to computers and wireless connections, that was a lesser concern than in past decades. From round-the-clock security patrols at ports during Operation Enduring Freedom in Afghanistan to the harbor and shoreside security patrols near the military prison at Guantanamo Bay, reservists bring many civilian skills to the Coast Guard. They often perform office work, helping as dental assistants, mechanics, and galley cooks, allowing active-duty Coasties to focus on rescue and security. In 2006, Coast Guard reservists serving in nearly every rank and rate were deployed to various strategic ports in Kuwait.

The Coast Guard Auxiliary

Auxiliarists are an all-volunteer arm of the Coast Guard that also allow for greater efficiency and education of the boating public. Founded in 1939, the Auxiliary is dedicated to teaching boating-safety courses and otherwise educating the public. In the past decade, their skills have allowed them to take on newer roles. Auxiliarists function much like the volunteers in a hospital providing much needed support during their faithful hours of duty. Standing watch, answering phones, teaching courses, flying their own aircraft, or piloting their own vessels as part of a search-and-rescue mission, their reliable, voluntary service makes these civilians an integral part of the Coast Guard family.

Ranks and Rates

So, what are ranks and rates? A rank is a Coastie's title and tells others where one fits into the order of the Coast Guard. As one increases in rank, responsibility, accountability, and the rate of pay increase. Enlisted ranks are the lowest, but by no means less important positions. One can move to the officer corps from the enlisted ranks through the warrant-officer program or by qualifying for ensign when one is a second class petty officer, or by qualifying for Officer Candidate School.

Coast Guard Jobs

Jobs in the Coast Guard are called rates and are separate from rank. One can virtually be almost any rank in almost any rate as his or her career progresses. For example, a food-service technician prepares and serves food to fellow Coast Guardsmen and women. Many Coast Guard careers have direct counterparts in the civilian (nonmilitary) world.

Coast Guard Jobs

Some of the jobs available to enlisted men and women in the Coast Guard are shown below.

- **aviation-survival technician**—Inspects, services, and repairs aircraft and provides safety training.
- **Boatswain's mate**—Masters of seamanship service on all types of Coast Guard ships.
- **damage controlman**—Welds and cuts metal for repairs; fights fires; repairs plumbing, buildings, and ships; and helps detect and decontaminate chemical and biological weapons.
- **electrician's mate**—Installs, maintains, and repairs electrical equipment.
- **electronics technician**—Maintains and repairs electronics, radios, radar, computer, and navigation equipment.
- **food-service specialist**—Prepares food at stations and on ships.
- **gunner's mate**—Specialists in small arms, including pistols, rifles, machine guns, and 76mm guns.
- **health-services technician**—Provides health care services for Coasties.
- **machinery technician**—Operates and maintains all types of Coast Guard machinery.
- **marine-science technician**—Investigates pollution and oversees pollution cleanups; patrols harbors for safety and security; boards foreign vessels to enforce pollution and navigation laws.
- **musician**—Plays in United States Coast Guard Band.
- **port-security specialist**—Protects American ports.
- **storekeeper**—Responsible for clothing, parts, and other supplies.

Ranks and Salaries of Enlisted Coasties

		Enlisted	
Rank	**Pay Grade**	**Approximate Salary***	**Insignia**
Seaman Recruit	E-1	under 4 months: $1,175 per month over 4 months: $1,270 per month	No insignia
Seaman Apprentice	E-2	$17,100 per year	
Seaman	E-3	$18,000–20,400 per year**	
Third Class Petty Officer	E-4	$19,200–24,000 per year	
Second Class Petty Officer	E-5	$21,600–30,000 per year	
First Class Petty Officer	E-6	$24,000–36,000 per year	
Chief Petty Officer	E-7	$27,600–49,200 per year	
Senior Chief Petty Officer	E-8	$39,600–55,200 per year	
Master Chief Petty Officer	E-9	$48,000–64,800 per year	

* Approximate salaries are as of 2006 and do not include food and housing allowances, free health care, money for college, and bonuses.
** Salary for ranks E-3 through E-9 depend on the number of years in service.

Ranks and Salaries of Officers

		Warrant Officers		
Rank	**Pay Grade**	**Approximate Salary per year***	**Insignia**	
Chief Warrant Officer 2	W-2	$32,100–52,500		
Chief Warrant Officer 3	W-3	$36,500–60,400		
Chief Warrant Officer 4	W-4	$39,900–69,700		
		Officers		
Ensign	O-1	$28,800–36,000		
Lieutenant, junior grade	O-2	$32,400–45,600		
Lieutenant	O-3	$38,400–62,400		
Lieutenant Commander	O-4	$43,200–73,200		
Commander	O-5	$50,400–86,400		
Captain	O-6	$61,200–105,600		
Rear Admiral (lower half)	O-7	$82,800–120,000		
Rear Admiral (upper half)	O-8	$99,600–135,600		
Vice Admiral	O-9	$140,400–$150,000		
Admiral	O-10	$160,800–$170,400		

* Salaries are as of 2006 and do not include food and housing allowances, free health care, money for college, and bonuses; also, an approximate salary range has been given for each rank.

This allows Coasties to transfer their skills to new jobs when they leave the service.

The Coast Guard Band

Formed in 1925, the United States Coast Guard Band has been one of the five premier military service bands ever since. Stationed at the Coast Guard Academy in New London, Connecticut, members are graduates of renowned music academies. One of the most respected military bands in the world, the Coast Guard band performs at such prestigious venues as the John F. Kennedy Center for the Performing Arts in Washington, D.C., and Lincoln Center and Carnegie Hall in New York City. Routinely touring throughout the United States, it has also performed overseas. The band

A member of the Coast Guard Band plays the clarinet.

also provides National Public Radio with recordings for broadcasts, and members have recorded CDs. The band has performed at every presidential inauguration since 1928.

Critters of the Coast Guard

The presence of animals allows crews to develop camaraderie and share a common bond. Reducing the stress of long deployments and improving morale with their unexpected antics, friendly or curious animals have been adopted by many Coast Guard crews. Birds, goats, dogs, bears, and even a penguin have provided a unique kind of companionship for Coasties away from home.

A dog called Sinbad was arguably the most famous Coast Guard mascot. Serving aboard the cutter *Campbell*, Sinbad had his own service record and uniform, and he even had a book written about him: *Sinbad of the Coast Guard* by George R. Foley. Other animals provided entertainment and laughter for Coasties patrolling the high seas. They include:

- **Penguin:** emperor penguin in Antarctica; mascot of the cutter *Eastwind* during Operation Deep Freeze I.
- **Goat:** mascot of Coast Guard cutter *Perry*; he earned two awards.
- **Bear:** mascot of the cutter *Thetis*, famous for being largest mascot in Coast Guard history.

- **Charlie, a California harbor seal:** sang or barked for his supper at the Los Angeles harbor lighthouse in the 1960s.
- **Maximilian Talisman, a dog:** enlisted in 1950 and retired in 1957 aboard the cutter *Klamath*; earned the United Nations medal, the Korean Service Medal, and the National Defense Service Medal.
- **Munro, a dog:** assigned to Sector Field Office Moriches; named after the Coast Guard's only Medal of Honor recipient.

Sinbad, a mascot of the Coast Guard, appeared in a U.S. Army publication dated January 23, 1944.

A Seagoing Service

As of 2005, about thirty-nine thousand men and women comprised the United States Coast Guard's active duty forces. An additional 8,100 reservists swelled the ranks a bit, while 7,000 civilians worked for the Coast Guard filling a wide range of positions. These critical employees provide a richness and diversity of skills, background, and experience.[1]

Women and Minorities

Today, the Coast Guard is a diverse military family. Women and minorities have worked through history to gain their rightful place in the ranks of the Coast Guard.

African Americans

From the earliest days of the Revenue Cutter Service until 1843, African-American slaves were forced to serve in the Coast Guard as stewards, cooks, and seamen. In 1865, the slaves were freed by the Thirteenth Amendment to the Constitution. Free African Americans joined the Revenue Cutter Service. In 1875, the Life-Saving Service employed more than twenty-five African Americans at life-saving stations on the eastern seaboard. The only all-black crew in the history of the Coast Guard operated Station 17 at Pea Island, North Carolina. While all were freed slaves, its keeper, Richard Etheridge, was also a Civil War veteran. When an

▲ Captain Michael A. "Roaring" Healy was the first commissioned African-American officer of the United States government and the first to command a U.S. warship.

all-white crew refused to serve under his leadership, he appointed an all-black crew, all of whom saved men, women, and children in many daring rescues.

However, it was not until 1887 that Captain Michael A. "Roaring" Healy became the only African American to command a cutter before the formal creation of the Coast Guard. From 1887 to 1895, Healy served as commanding officer of the cutter *Bear*, catching illegal seal hunters, bringing medical supplies to Alaskans, preparing navigational charts, and documenting ice and weather reports. When Healy retired, he had achieved the third-highest officer rank in the Revenue Cutter Service.

The Pea Island Crew in Action

When a hurricane struck the Outer Banks of North Carolina in 1896, the African-American crew at Pea Island managed to save everyone aboard the shipwrecked E.S. *Newman*. When Richard Etheridge and his crew arrived on scene, the conditions prohibited use of their rescue equipment. By ingeniously tying lines around two Pea Island crew members, the lifesavers could alternate and make eight separate swims out to the ship and rescue

Richard Etheridge, at left, and his crew pose in front of their Pea Island station in 1896.

Alex Haley, Chief Journalist

In 1939, Alex Haley enlisted in the Coast Guard as a mess cook and steward for the officer's mess, the only rates open to African Americans at the time. While at sea, he wrote dozens of letters and received replies, earning him status as an accomplished letter writer, and became known for his ability to write interesting stories.

By 1944, Haley was assigned to edit *Our Post*, the official Coast Guard publication. The next year, he won the Ship's Editorial Association Award and served as an assistant to the public relations officer at Coast Guard Headquarters until 1959. The Coast Guard created the rank of Chief Journalist for Haley, and he focused on writing stories to promote the Coast Guard for the media. Following a twenty-year Coast Guard career, including battle experience in World War II and the Korean War, Haley retired in 1959. But he held a special fondness for the Coast Guard: "It's a small service, and there's a lot of esprit de corps."[1]

Haley continued to write professionally, and he cowrote the *Autobiography of Malcolm X*. In 1977, his book *Roots: The Saga of an American Family*, about an American's search to discover his African ancestors was turned into a television miniseries seen by more than 130 million viewers.

Haley died on February 10, 1992, but continues to serve as a role model for Coasties, especially those in the public affairs rate whose annual writing awards are named after him.

passengers in the pounding surf and blustery conditions. One of Etheridge's men, Theodore Meekins, having served for some forty-one years, eventually drowned during a particularly tough rescue. His son went on to be a Coast Guard pilot, and his grandson serves as a prevention officer in the Coast Guard.

One hundred years later, the Pea Island crew was posthumously awarded Gold lifesaving medals for heroic feats. While Etheridge died in 1900, Pea Island remained an all-black life-saving station for fifty more years.

The twentieth and twenty-first centuries saw African Americans taking on more and more roles in the Coast Guard. In 1945, the first five African-American women joined SPARs, a female division of the Coast Guard.

Today, African Americans are an integral part of the efficient lifesaving and security force that they helped build.

American Indians

Since 1887, American Indians have also served the Coast Guard. They first comprised a lifesaving-station crew at Neah Bay, Washington. American Indians also served in the U.S. Lighthouse Service before the creation of the U.S. Coast Guard. Through the twentieth and twenty-first centuries, American Indians have continued their important service in the Coast Guard.

Latinos

Latinos achieved success in the Coast Guard as lighthouse keepers in the 1800s and early 1900s. They also served in the Revenue Cutter Service and the U.S. Life-Saving Service. In 1920, Mess Attendant First Class Arthur Flores and Seaman John Gomez were awarded the Silver Lifesaving Medal for heroism for saving survivors of the schooner *Isaiah K. Stetson*, which sank off the coast of Massachusetts.

Latinos continued their service through World War II and the many conflicts of the twentieth century. Today, they are an important part of the U.S. Coast Guard.

For retired Master Chief Petty Officer Luis Diaz, a varied perspective has helped him enjoy a long career as a reservist—twenty-two years on active duty and six years as a civilian public-affairs officer in Miami, Florida. He was the first Puerto Rican to reach the ranks of chief petty officer, senior chief petty officer, and master chief petty officer, and said there are many opportunities in the Coast Guard. When he was a civilian, Diaz was told not to speak Spanish at work, but now he acts as an interpreter in the Coast Guard. A veteran of many important military operations, including Vietnam while in the Navy, he worked on the 1994 mass exodus of Haitian and Cuban immigrants and many hurricane operations.

Asians

Like Latinos, Asians also have a history of serving their country in the U.S. Lighthouse Service, especially in the early 1900s. During World War II (from 1941 to 1945) Florence Ebersole Smith Finch, a Filipino, became the only SPAR to receive the Pacific Campaign ribbon. As part of the war effort, Finch smuggled food into the island's prison camps during World War II before being captured, beaten, and tortured in three prison camps. Rescued by American forces, she was one of only a handful of women to be awarded the U.S. Medal of Freedom.

Today, Asians in the Coast Guard continue the rich tradition started over a hundred years ago by their ancestors in the U.S. Lighthouse Service.

Women

As early as the 1830s, women officially served as lighthouse keepers in the Lighthouse Service. In 1942, SPAR was

---

CAREER PROFILE

Vice Commandant, Vivien S. Crea

The first female to serve as second in command of a military service, Vice Admiral Vivien S. Crea has achieved the rank of vice commandant. Her resume includes a stint as the first female air-station commander and commander, Atlantic Area and Maritime Defense Zone. She is one of only a few pilots to have flown the C-130 Hercules, the H-65 Dolphin helicopter, and the Gulfstream II jet. Crea also served as the first female Coast Guard aide to President Ronald Reagan.

Vice Admiral Crea has earned four Legion of Merit awards, the Defense Superior Service Medal, and the Meritorious Service Medal. Crea holds master's degrees from Central Michigan University and from the Massachusetts Institute of Technology.

▲ Coast Guard SPARs who served in World War II gathered at Marinette, Wisconsin, to witness the christening of the Coast Guard Cutter *Spar*. Pictured are prospective commanding officer of *Spar*, Lieutenant Commander Joanna Nunan (left front), and SPARs Betty Splaine (center front) and Lorraine Dieterle (right front). The attorney general at the time, Janet Reno (center right, in back), christened the ship.

founded and was an important contribution to the war effort in Word War II. The group was deactivated in 1947, but the U.S. Coast Guard Women's Volunteer Reserve began in January 1950.

In 1973, the Women's Reserve ended and women were given active-duty status in the Coast Guard. Two years later, some began to train as pilots. By 1976, the Coast Guard Academy became the first armed service academy to admit women.

The Right Equipment

Whether a man, woman, white, black, Asian, Latino, or American Indian, each Coastie must have the right equipment and vehicles to navigate the air and sea. Good technology helps Coast Guard crews fulfill their important missions for the United States.

Coast Guard Districts

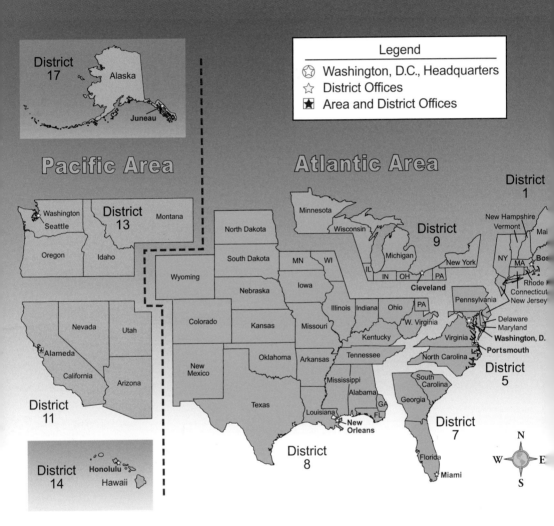

The area the Coast Guard is responsible for is divided into nine districts. There once were more districts but some were combined, which is why districts 2, 3, 4, 6, 10, 12, 15, and 16 no longer exist.

Eight

Cutters, Boats, and Planes

Meticulous and thorough training in aircraft, on boats, and shoreside allow Coast Guard crews to provide expertise to the American public in a variety of ways. Therefore, whether providing water-based support to NASA missions at Cape Canaveral or critical hurricane disaster relief, the Coast Guard's skills remind the public of those brave surfmen and women who serve valiantly along America's coasts.

Pilots fly critical missions for the Coast Guard using C-130s, HH-60 Jayhawks, and HH-65 Dolphin helicopters. A recent addition to the Coast Guard is the Helicopter Interdiction Tactical Squadron (HITRON) unit, the Coast Guard's first and only airborne law-enforcement unit trained and authorized for the airborne use of force.

U.S. Coast Guard Cutters

When the R.M.S. *Titanic* collided with an iceberg on April 15, 1912, more than fifteen hundred lives were lost at sea. That tragic loss of life immediately increased awareness of ice hazards in the ocean. Initially, the Navy assigned two ships for patrol, but then ran short on manpower. In 1914, when the Safety of Life at Sea (SOLAS) Treaty was signed by the world's great maritime powers, the Coast Guard, a natural lead agency for maintaining the safe flow of commerce, was given responsibility for ice patrol from the Chesapeake Bay to Maine. On the Great Lakes where seven navigable waterways are ordinarily filled with cargo ships, ice breaking became a priority to keep shipping channels open.

The Coast Guard also uses a variety of boats and aircraft. A cutter is any boat at least 65-feet long, with room for a crew to live on board. Cutters usually have smaller boats on board and Polar Class icebreakers carry an Arctic Survey Boat (ASB) and Landing Craft.

Polar Class Icebreakers

The Polar Class icebreakers are among the largest U.S. Coast Guard cutters. Each is 399 feet long. These ships have been specifically designed for open-water ice breaking and have reinforced hulls, special ice-breaking bows, and a system that makes ice breaking a lot easier to do. The *Polar Sea* and *Polar Star* were built in the 1970s. They serve science and research teams in the Arctic and Antarctic areas, as well as provide supplies to out of-the-way stations. In the polar regions, heavy icebreakers

▲ Ensign Jessica Barbeau plots a course on the *Polar Star*, a 399-foot Polar Class icebreaker.

have been the only surface ships capable of creating a safe channel to resupply scientific and military stations in Antarctica and the Arctic. The Polar Class ships have also responded to oil spills and search-and-rescue cases, and they have helped expand our understanding of heavy ice and its impact on navigation. The International Ice Patrol has used aircraft to locate the boundaries of the ice field, thus saving lives and money for international shipping companies and the international field of commerce.

Training Barque *Eagle*

The *Eagle* is a 295-foot three-masted sailing barque. It is located at the Coast Guard Academy in New

▲ Third Class Cadet Tracey Swaynos smiles at the helm of the *Eagle*.

London, Connecticut. It is the only active (operational) commissioned sailing vessel in the U.S. services. It is one of five such training barques in the world. The others are located in Romania, Portugal, Germany, and Russia.

The *Eagle*'s name pre-dates the founding of the United States Coast Guard. The first *Eagle* was commissioned in 1792, just two years after the founding of the Revenue Marine, the forerunner of today's Coast Guard.

Today, the *Eagle* can serve about 175 cadets and instructors from the U.S. Coast Guard Academy at a time. Cadets are taught seamanship on its decks.

On the teak decks and rugged rigging of the *Eagle*, male and female cadets are first confronted with sea challenges. From this experience they develop a respect for the wind, waves, and weather they will likely face in the Coast Guard. Each drill and exercise is designed to test the limits of their endurance. They learn to conquer any fear they may have. The training cadets receive on this

The Cutter Fleet

Some other cutters in the U.S. Coast Guard include:

- 420-foot icebreakers
- 378-foot high endurance cutters
- 290-foot inland icebreakers
- medium endurance cutters (from 210 feet to 282 feet)
- 225-foot and 180-foot seagoing buoy tenders
- 160-foot, 100-foot, and 75-foot inland construction tenders
- 140-foot icebreaking tug
- 87-foot coastal patrol boat
- 75-foot and 65-foot river buoy tenders
- 100-foot and 65-foot inland buoy tenders
- 65-foot small harbor tug

sailing vessel has greatly helped them during their Coast Guard careers. Cadets have a chance to apply navigation and engineering training received in classes at the academy. As upper class cadets, they perform junior-officer leadership roles. As under-class cadets, they act as the crew of the *Eagle*. They watch the helm and steer the vessel using the giant brass and wood wheels. This allows them to try Coast Guard duties from all perspectives.

More than two hundred lines of rigging must be coordinated during a major ship maneuver, so cadets must learn the name and function of each line. The steel hull of the *Eagle* is almost half an inch thick. The *Eagle* moves easily through water reaching a top speed of 17 knots (about 19.5 miles per hour). At the Coast Guard Academy, the *Eagle* berths on the Thames River in Connecticut. About one thousand cadets a year will sail aboard the *Eagle*.

Coastal Buoy Tender

The 175-foot Keeper-class coastal buoy tenders represent advances in buoy tending. All of the ships in this class are named after lighthouse keepers. They are the first Coast Guard cutters that have special propulsion units instead of the standard propeller and rudder. They can rotate 360 degrees. Combined with a thruster in the bow, the new propulsion units allow the Keeper-class cutters to maneuver in the water like never before. This is

▲ Crew members of the *Maria Bray*—a 175-foot coastal buoy tender based out of Mayport, Florida—work to bring on deck a buoy that weighs over 15,000 pounds on June 24, 2004.

important because they need to check buoys, which help show ships safe passages through coastal waters. If the buoys are in the wrong place, a ship could hit a reef, the ocean floor, or other obstruction, possibly causing damage and endangering the lives of those on board.

The coastal buoy tenders' state-of-the-art electronics and navigation systems use a Differential Global Positioning System. As a result, these cutters maneuver and position buoys more accurately and efficiently while requiring fewer Coast Guardsmen and women to operate them.

Patrol Boats

Island-class 110-foot patrol boats are similar to a type of British patrol boat. All the boats in the Island-class boats are named after U.S. islands. With the ability to go long distances, these boats replaced the older 95-foot Cape-class patrol boats. These cutters have advanced electronics and navigation equipment.

Coast Guard Small Boats

Small boats usually operate near shore and on inland waterways. They are smaller than cutters, ranging in size from twelve to sixty-four feet in length.

Motor Lifeboat

The forty-seven-foot motor lifeboat is meant to be used for rescues in high seas, surf, and heavy weather.

It can be used in a rescue at sea even under the most difficult conditions. It is almost unsinkable because it is built not to tip over in high waves and crews can rid themselves of, or bail out, any water that gets into the boat. This updated lifeboat is the replacement for the aging forty-four-foot motor lifeboat.

Deployable Pursuit Boat

The thirty-eight-foot deployable pursuit boat (DPB) is used often in the Caribbean Sea and Eastern Pacific. Most of the cocaine smuggled through those areas travels on "go-fasts," thirty- to forty-foot high-speed craft, that carry 2,200 to 4,400 pounds of illegal narcotics. Working with other Coast Guard

These deployable pursuit boats speed down the Elizabeth River in Virginia.

ships and aircraft, deployable pursuit boat crews stop and board "go-fasts," significantly reducing the flow of drugs to the United States.

Rigid Hull Inflatable Boat

Rigid hull inflatable boats have reinforced plastic hulls that can float easily. They are powered by either a gasoline motor or a diesel engine. These boats can be easily deployed from a Coast Guard cutter. The Rigid Hull Inflatable Boat can be used as part of all types of Coast Guard missions. Its small size and ruggedness make this possible.

▼ Crewmembers of this rigid hull inflatable boat practice high-speed tactics off the coast of Camp Lejeune, North Carolina on March 3, 2003.

▲ An HC-130 Hercules flies over North Carolina.

Coast Guard Aircraft

Coast Guard aircraft are used for search and rescue, law enforcement, environmental response, ice operations, and pursuit of smugglers. Coast Guard airplanes operate from air stations, while helicopters operate from flight-deck-equipped cutters, air stations, and air facilities.

HC-130 Hercules Airplane

The C-130J Hercules is the newest generation of tactical military transport aircraft. It has integrated digital controls with head-up displays, new propulsion system, and other major upgrades that reduce costs

▲ Lieutenant Jeanine McIntosh, a Coast Guard pilot, sits at the controls of her C-130 Hercules aircraft.

and crew size while offering great performance improvements. The aircraft is used for all of the Coast Guard's primary mission areas: long-range search and rescue, law enforcement (alien-migrant capture and counter-drug operations), airlift, and homeland security. The C-130J climbs faster and higher than its predecessors and flies farther at a higher cruise speed.

HH-60 Jayhawk Helicopter

The United States Coast Guard has forty-two medium-range Sikorsky HH-60 Jayhawk helicopters in its fleet. The Jayhawk's state-of-the-art radar, radio, and navigational equipment enables the helicopter to carry out search and rescue, law enforcement, military readiness, and marine environmental-protections missions.

The Jayhawk uses the NAVSTAR global positioning system as its primary long-range navigational aid. On board the Jayhawk, the Collins RCVR-3A radio receives data from four of the system's eighteen worldwide satellites at the same time, pinpointing the helicopter's position. With its two engines, the Jayhawk can fly three hundred miles offshore, remain on scene forty-five minutes, hoist six people on board, and return to its point of origin with a safe fuel reserve. Normal cruising speeds of 135 knots can be increased to a "dash" velocity of 180 knots when necessary.

▲ A rescue swimmer hangs from an HH-60 Jayhawk helicopter as the crew from Air Station Cape Cod performs a search-and-rescue demonstration for people enjoying Fleet Week festivities in New York City on May 27, 2006.

HH-65 Dolphin Helicopter

As of August 2006, the Coast Guard had ninety-four short-range HH-65A helicopters.[1] These twin-engine Dolphins operate up to 150 miles offshore and will fly comfortably at 150 knots for about three hours.

Though normally stationed ashore, the Dolphins can be carried on board medium- and high-endurance Coast Guard cutters. They assist in the missions of search and rescue, enforcement of laws and treaties including drug law enforcement, polar ice breaking, marine environmental protection including pollution control, and military readiness.

Helicopters stationed aboard icebreakers are the ship's eyes in finding thinner and more navigable ice channels. They fly reconnaissance and airlift supplies to ships and to villages isolated by winter ice.

The HH-65A's minimum equipment requirements exceed anything previously packaged into one helicopter weighing less than ten thousand pounds. HH-65As are made with many different types of materials mixed together, called a composite. The composite material is corrosion resistant.

Another unique feature of the Dolphin is its computerized flight-management system, which integrates state-of-the-art communication and navigation equipment. This system provides

▲ Five HH-65 Dolphin helicopters sit ready in a hangar in northern Michigan.

automatic flight control. At the pilot's direction, the system will bring the aircraft to a stable hover fifty feet above a selected object. This is an important feature in darkness or inclement weather. Selected search patterns can be flown automatically, freeing the pilot and copilot to concentrate on sighting the search target.

MH-68A Stingray Helicopter

The MH-68A is specially equipped with infrared sensors and night-vision goggles, and is armed with M16 rifles and M240 machine guns mounted on the doors. It also has an RC-50 laser-sighted .50 caliber rifle. Based in Jacksonville, Florida, these

An MH-68A helicopter flies a homeland security patrol over New York City in April 2003. The MH-68A fleet is based in Jacksonville, Florida.

helicopters can cruise at speeds in excess of one hundred miles per hour, making them one of the fastest choppers in the air. This makes them a sleek, high-tech law enforcement tool that can outrun drug and migrant smugglers, but they are also a critical line of homeland defense. The aircraft were made shipboard compatible. Night shipboard landings, now operational procedures Coast Guard-wide, were first done with the Stingray.

Nine

The Future Burns Bright

The Coast Guard has focused on four mission areas: maritime law enforcement and military operations, marine safety, environmental protection, and homeland security. This armed service protects and defends American coastal and inland waterways while ensuring the safety of our ports and protecting the flow of commerce.

Crew members work to uphold environmental laws that protect marine mammals, seabirds, and fish. The men and women of the Coast Guard work hard to prevent drug smugglers and illegal migrants from reaching American shores. Law enforcement, coastal border protection, the safe flow of commerce, and lifesaving missions all blend together to make the Coast Guard a world-renowned protector of the coast. Search-and-rescue crews are often on the lookout for homeland security threats. Using advanced technology such as underwater robots, voiceless vessel transmissions, and advanced aircraft that can sense oil as it floats on water, today's Coast Guard is a skilled and flexible force.

Balancing America's changing security needs with protection of the marine environment and saving lives at sea has its foundations in the ever-changing needs of our country and the international community. Though more commonly known for work along the nation's 95,000 miles of coastline, the Coast Guard also works on navigable rivers and waterways and maintains safety within 360 primary ports.[1] A lengthy maritime military tradition coupled with expertise in rescue, security, and law

▲ U.S. Coast Guard Petty Officer Third Class Charles Carver patrols New York harbor on Dec. 22, 2003, after the Department of Homeland Security raised the nation's threat level to orange.

enforcement places greater importance on Coast Guard work than ever before. The Coast Guard enforces U.S. laws, international treaties, and maritime transportation laws as well as provides security at ports, waterways, and shore facilities. Because of this, it is the lead agency for homeland defense. The Coast Guard also leads ice-breaking missions and protects the marine environment by enforcing fishery regulations, often transporting scientists to the North and South poles.

New missions call for new programs and technology. At the center of the Coast Guard's future plans are two massive programs that allow the armed service to transform itself into a modern-day military service.

Deepwater

The Deepwater program allows the Coast Guard to upgrade and purchase its fleet of aircraft and ships. Unmanned aerial vehicles (UAVs) will be on board cutters to allow for long-range reconnaissance missions, which will help the Coast Guard to better plan missions at sea. Bigger ships carrying UAVs and helicopters will be able to remain at sea for longer deployments, using smaller crews.

Rescue 21

Command and control systems allow the military to talk to, track, and direct units. Rescue 21 is a cutting-edge design that uses digital position tracking and

▲ The offshore-patrol cutter (computer illustration pictured), will be part of the Coast Guard's Deepwater fleet.

allows the Coast Guard to talk directly to other first responders in an emergency. It helps the Coast Guard pinpoint the location of boaters in trouble while also allowing it to track its own boats.

A reserve force of about eighty-one hundred[2] will continue to shore up the regular active duty force while about thirty-three thousand auxiliarists perform vital vessel inspections, boating-safety classes, and aircraft and vessel patrols.[3] The Coast Guard will continue to be relied on for its expertise in

Fred's Place

Born of a need to intertwine the entire Coast Guard family, Fredsplace.org (see p. 124 for full Web address) connects people to information. That is nothing new for Fred Siegel, a retired chief warrant officer with a background steeped in telecommunications. Building a computer site for old shipmates in 1995 was cutting-edge use of the information superhighway. Used to getting the word out, Fred capitalizes on "word of mouse" to link Coasties to benefits, Coasties to Coasties, and Coasties to news. Now a part of the military.com umbrella, the Web site provides a relaxed conversational mode for sharing information, much as Fred did in his years as a chief petty officer.

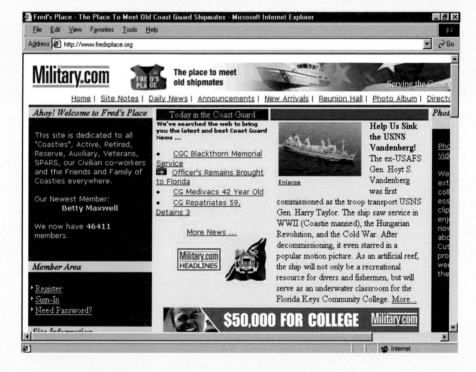

▲ Fred Siegel created Fred's Place so that veterans of the Coast Guard could have a site to find news about the Coast Guard and to connect with old friends from the service.

search and rescue as well as law-enforcement protection of ports and other interests involving commerce. Combating terrorism, ensuring port and cargo safety, and battling drug smugglers, polluters, and illegal migrants will all continue to pose challenges in a changing world.

Coast Guard Motto and Song

The Coast Guard motto is "Semper Paratus," meaning "Always Ready." It is also the name of the Coast Guard song, written in 1922 by Captain Francis von Boskerk while aboard the cutter *Yamacraw*. The song was updated in 1927 and again in 1969:

First Verse

> From Aztec shore to Arctic zone,
> To Europe and Far East,
> The Flag is carried by our ships,
> In times of war and peace,
> And never have we struck it yet,
> In spite of foe-men's might,
> Who cheered our crews and cheered again,
> For showing how to fight.

Chorus

> We're always ready for the call,
> We place our trust in Thee,
> Through surf and storm and howling gale,
> High shall our purpose be.
> "*Semper paratus*" is our guide,
> Our fame, our glory too,
> To fight to save, or fight to die,
> Aye! Coast Guard we are for you!

1790

1798–1800

Revenue
Cutter Service,
1790–1915

1716—British colonists begin building lighthouses in America.

August 4, 1790—At the prompting of Secretary of the Treasury Alexander Hamilton, the first version of the U.S. Coast Guard, the Revenue Cutter Service, is created by a tariff act.

March 21, 1791—Hopley Yeaton becomes the first commissioned officer of the Revenue Cutter Service after being appointed by President George Washington.

1798–1800—Coast Guard participates in the Quasi War with France, during which the *Pickering* captured ten enemy chips.

1808–1865—Revenue Cutter Service combats the illegal slave trade.

1812–1815—War of 1812.

June 12, 1813—Revenue Cutter Service ship *Surveyor* is captured by the British frigate *Narcissus*.

1822—Helps enforce ban on the cutting of live oak trees in Florida.

1832—Secretary of the Treasury Louis McLane orders Revenue Cutter Service to assist mariners during the winter.

1836–1839—Revenue Cutter Service aids in the fight against Seminole Indians in Florida.

1837—Lifesaving becomes the core mission of the Revenue Cutter Service.

1843—African-American slaves no longer forced to serve in the Coast Guard.

1846–1848—The Revenue Cutter Service assists the U.S. Marine Corps in ship-to-shore battles during the Mexican-American War.

1848—Volunteer lifesaving stations are present on the Atlantic and Pacific coasts, the Gulf of Mexico coast, and the coasts of the Great Lakes.

1846–1848

1854—U.S. government begins paying Life-Saving Service station keepers.

1861–1865—The American Civil War.

April 11, 1861—The cutter *Harriet Lane* fires first maritime shots in Civil War.

1871—Sumner Kimball becomes chief of the Revenue Marine Service and the first superintendent of the Life-Saving Service.

1861

1876—Academy is founded for the Revenue Cutter Service; it will become the Coast Guard Academy.

1878—The Life-Saving Service becomes independent from the Revenue Cutter Service.

1879—Ida Lewis becomes the official lighthouse keeper for the Lime Rock Lighthouse in Newport, Rhode Island.

1895—Captain Ellsworth Price Bertholf becomes first Revenue Cutter officer to attend the Naval War College.

1879

1896

1896—The all-African-American Pea Island crew distinguishes itself in the rescue of the E.S. *Newman.*

1898—Revenue Cutter Service helps with blockading and lifesaving efforts during the Spanish-American War.

1911—Ellsworth Price Bertholf named commandant of Revenue Cutter Service.

1915—Life-Saving Service and Revenue Cutter Service are combined to become the U.S. Coast Guard on January 28; Ellsworth Price Bertholf is appointed first commandant of the U.S. Coast Guard; there are 285 Life-Saving Service stations around the United States.

1915

1917–1918—Coast Guard escorts American vessels during World War I.

1920s—Helps fight illegal alcohol traffickers during Prohibition; Coast Guard aviation program expands.

1925—Coast Guard Band is founded.

1926—Coast Guard builds its first icebreakers.

1928—Coast Guard Band performs at its first presidential inauguration.

1932

1932—New Coast Guard Academy is built in New London, Connecticut.

1935–1941—Coast Guard helps enforce Neutrality Act.

1937—U.S. Lighthouse Service officially becomes part of the U.S. Coast Guard.

1939—The Coast Guard Reserve and Auxiliary are created; Alex Haley enlists in the Coast Guard.

December 7, 1941—Coast Guard helps defend against Pearl Harbor attack.

1944

1941–1945—World War II.

1943—The Coast Guard women's reserve, SPAR, is created.

1945—The first five African-American women join SPAR.

1947—The barque *Eagle* is acquired, and is used to train Coast Guard Academy cadets to this day.

1950–1953—Coast Guard offers combat support during Korean War.

1965–1973

1965–1973—Helps patrol rivers and coastlines during the Vietnam War.

1967—Moves from Department of Commerce to Department of Transportation.

1973—Women are given active-duty status in the Coast Guard.

January 28, 1980—*Blackthorn* collides with an oil tanker, killing twenty-three Coast Guard crew members.

April–October 1980—Coast Guard provides security and lifesaving services during the Mariel Boatlift.

1980

1989

2004

1989—Assists in the cleanup of the *Exxon Valdez* oil spill.

September 11, 2001—Assists with marine and port security immediately after the September 11 attacks.

2003—On March 1, moves from Department of Transportation to become part of the newly created Department of Homeland Security; more than fifty-one hundred lives saved by Coast Guard teams.

2004—Provides security for Global G-8 Summit; on April 24, Petty Officer Third Class Nathan Bruckenthal becomes the first Coastie killed since the Vietnam War; Coast Guard helps in relief effort during a busy hurricane season.

August–September 2005—Provides search-and-rescue and security services during and in the aftermath of Hurricane Katrina.

Chapter 1. *Hurricane Heroics*

1. Personal interview with Petty Officer Josh Mitcheltree, March 1, 2006.

2. Ibid.

3. Ibid.

4. Ibid.

5. Ibid.

6. Ibid.

7. Ibid.

8. Ibid.

9. Ibid.

10. Ibid.

Chapter 2. *Guardians of the Sea*

1. Alexander Hamilton, *The Federalist Papers: The Federalist No. 12*, The University of Oklahoma: College of Law, November 27, 1787, <http://www.law.ou.edu/hist/federalist/federalist-10-19/federalist.12.shtml> (October 23, 2006).

2. "Historical Chronology," *U.S. Coast Guard*, n.d., <http://www.uscg.mil/hq/g-cp/comrel/factfile/Factcards/HistoricalChronology.html> (October 23, 2006).

3. "Surveyor, 1807," *U.S. Coast Guard*, May 2004, <http://www.uscg.mil/history/webcutters/surveyor%5F1807.html> (November 29, 2006).

4. *U.S. Coast Guard History*, <http://www.uscg.mil/history/h%5Fuslss.html> (December 2005).

5. "Ida Lewis," *U.S. Coast Guard*, January 2001, <http://www.uscg.mil/history/Ida%20Lewis%20Bio.html> (October 23, 2006).

Chapter 3. *Challenges and Successes*

1. Woodrow Wilson, "Primary Documents: U.S.

Declaration of War with Germany, 2 April 1917," *First World War.com*, April 14, 2002, <http://www.firstworldwar.com/source/usawardeclaration.htm> (October 24, 2006).

2. "Tampa History," *U.S. Coast Guard*, <http://www.uscg.mil/history/Tampa_1912.html> (August 4, 2006).

3. "The Coast Guard at War: National Security & Military Preparedness," *U.S. Coast Guard*. <http://www.uscg.mil/history/h_militaryindex.html> (October 4, 2006).

4. Kay M. Sheppard, "The Coastland Times," RootsWeb, 2004, <http://www.rootsweb.com/~nccurrit/obits/coastlandtimes.htm> (October 24, 2006).

5. "A History of Coast Guard Aviation: The Early Years (1915–1938)," *Coast Guard Aviation History*, 2003–2006, <http://uscgaviationhistory.aoptero.org/history01.html> (October 24, 2006).

6. "Neutrality Acts 1935–1941," January 21, 2000, <http://history.acusd.edu/gen/WW2timeline/neutralityacts.html> (October 24, 2006).

7. "Medal of Honor Inscription," *U.S. Coast Guard*, n.d., <http://www.uscg.mil/history/Munro%20Index.html> (August 4, 2006).

8. Dr. Robert M. Browning, Jr., "The Coast Guard At Iwo Jima," *U.S. Coast Guard*, n.d., <http://www.uscg.mil/history/IwoJima.html> (August 4, 2006).

9. Judith Silverstein, "Adrift," *U.S. Coast Guard: District 11 Public Affairs*, n.d., <http://www.uscgsanfrancisco.com/go/doc/586/89781/?printerfriendly=1> (October 24, 2006).

10. Brent Hurd, "America Remembers Unsung Heroes on Memorial Day," *Voice of America News*, May 31, 2005, <https://www.veteransadvantage.com/news/archive/AmericaRemembersUnsungHeroesOnMemorialDay.html> (October 24, 2006).

Chapter 4. *A Sea of Change*

1. Jonathan S. Wiarda, "The U.S. Coast Guard in Vietnam: Achieving Success in a Difficult War," *Naval War College Review*, Spring 1998, vol. LI, no. 2, <http://www.nwc.navy.mil/press/Review/1998/spring/art3-sp8.htm> (October 30, 2006).

2. Eugene N. Tulich, "The United States Coast Guard in South East Asia During the Vietnam Conflict," *U.S. Coast Guard*, April 1998, <http://www.uscg.mil/history/h_tulichvietnam.html> (October 30, 2006).

3. Jonathan S. Wiarda, "The U.S. Coast Guard in Vietnam: Achieving Success in a Difficult War."

4. Donald Canney, "The Coast Guard and the Environment," *U.S. Coast Guard*, October 2000, <http://www.uscg.mil/history/h_environment.html> (October 20, 2006).

5. PA3 Judy L. Silverstein, MSO Tampa, "Memories of Mariel: 20 Years Later," *U.S. Coast Guard*, n.d., <http://www.uscg.mil/reservist/mag2000/apr2000/mariel.htm> (November 29, 2006).

Chapter 5. *Changes in the Air*

1. "Homeland Security Subcommittee Hearing on the Transportation Security Administration and U.S. Coast Guard Budget Overview: Testimony of Admiral Thomas H. Collins, Commandant, U.S. Coast Guard," *United States Senate Committee on Appropriations: Hearings and Testimony*, March 23, 2004, <http://appropriations.senate.gov/hearmarkups/record.cfm?id=219472> (November 1, 2006).

2. VADM Harry G. Hamlet, USCG, "Creed of the United States Coast Guardsman," *U.S. Coast Guard*, December 1997, <http://www.uscg.mil/history/faqs/creed.html> (January 31, 2007).

Chapter 6. *The Faces of the Coast Guard*

1. "Personnel Statistics," *U.S. Coast Guard Fact File*,

June 2005, <http://www.uscg.mil/hq/g-cp/comrel/factfile/index.htm> (November 1, 2006).

Chapter 7. *Women and Minorities*

1. "USCGC Alex Haley Historical Information," *U.S. Coast Guard*, September 23, 2006, <http://www.uscg.mil/pacarea/haley/noframes/history.html> (November 1, 2006).

Chapter 8. *Cutters, Boats, and Planes*

1. "HH-65A 'Dolphin' Short Range Recovery Helicopter," *U.S. Coast Guard*, August 30, 2006, <http://www.uscg.mil/datasheet/hh-65.htm> (November 1, 2006).

Chapter 9. *The Future Burns Bright*

1. "Remarks by Secretary of Homeland Security Tom Ridge at the Port of Portland," *Department of Homeland Security*, April 5, 2004, <http://www.dhs.gov/xnews/speeches/speech_0162.shtm> (November 1, 2006).

2. "Personnel Statistics," *U.S. Coast Guard Fact File*, June 2005, <http://www.uscg.mil/hq/g-cp/comrel/factfile/index.htm> (November 1, 2006).

3. "Coast Guard Auxiliary at a Glance," *U.S. Coast Guard*, n.d., <http://www.uscg.mil/hq/g-cp/comrel/factfile/factcards/AuxGlance.html> (November 1, 2006).

bow—The front, or pointy end, of a boat.

bridge—Control room for an engine-powered ship, and place from which the ship is steered.

charts—Maps.

coxswain—Enlisted person in charge of a boat.

cutter—A vessel that is 65 feet or longer with accommodations for the crew.

deck—Nautical term for floor.

flare—Safety device that can be lit so you can be seen, if in trouble.

galley—Ship's kitchen.

helm—The wheel or tiller that controls the rudder.

homeported—City where a military ship is based.

hull—The main shell of a vessel.

knot—How speed is measured at sea.

port—To the left of the centerline when facing forward.

rudder—A board-shaped piece attached to the back of a ship or boat for steering and maneuvering.

Further Reading

Coast Guard History

Rindge, Ronald L. *WWII Homeland Defense: U.S. Coast Guard Beach Patrol in Malibu, 1942–1944*. Cayucos, Calif.: Ron and Sue Rindge, 2003.

Wright, David and David Zoby. *Fire on the Beach: Recovering the Lost Story of Richard Etheridge and the Pea Island Lifesavers*. New York: Oxford University Press, 2002.

Coast Guard Rescues

Demarest, Chris L. *Mayday! Mayday!: A Coast Guard Rescue*. New York: Margaret K. McElderry Books, 2004.

Lyons, Lewis. *Rescue at Sea with the U.S. and Canadian Coast Guards*. Broomall, Pa.: Mason Crest Publishers, 2003.

Coast Guard Vehicles

Braulick, Carrie A. *U.S. Coast Guard Cutters*. Mankato, Minn.: Capstone Press, 2007.

Goldberg, Jan. *The C-130 Hercules*. New York: Rosen Central, 2003.

Holden, Henry M. *Coast Guard Rescue and Patrol Aircraft*. Berkeley Heights, N.J.: Enslow Publishers, Inc., 2002.

Stone, Lynn M. *Coast Guard Cutters*. Vero Beach, Fla.: Rourke, 2006.

———. *HH-60 Pave Hawk*. Vero Beach, Fla.: Rourke, 2006.

Other Books on the Coast Guard

Benson, Michael. *The U.S. Coast Guard*. Minneapolis, Minn.: Lerner Publications Company, 2005.

Braulick, Carrie A. *The U.S. Coast Guard*. Mankato, Minn.: Capstone Press, 2005.

Green, Michael. *The United States Coast Guard*. Mankato, Minn.: Capstone Books, 2000.

Keeter, Hunter. *The U.S. Homeland Security Forces*. Milwaukee, Wis.: World Almanac Library, 2005.

Lurch, Bruno. *United States Coast Guard*. Chicago, Ill.: Heinemann Library, 2004.

Roza, Greg. *Careers in the Coast Guard's Search and Rescue Unit*. New York: Rosen Publishing Group, Inc., 2003.

Weintraub, Aileen. *Life Inside the Coast Guard Academy*. New York: Children's Press, 2002.

Fred's Place: A Place to Meet Old Shipmates
<http://www.fredsplace.org>

U.S. Coast Guard
<http://www.uscg.mil/default.asp>

U.S. Coast Guard Academy
<http://www.cga.edu/>

U.S. Coast Guard Recruiting Web Site
<http://www.gocoastguard.com/>